No Soul Left Behind

Edgar Cayce books by A. Robert Smith

My Life as a Seer: The Lost Memoirs

No Soul Left Behind: The Words and Wisdom of Edgar Cayce

Hugh Lynn Cayce: About My Father's Business

No Soul Left Behind

THE WORDS AND WISDOM OF EDGAR CAYCE

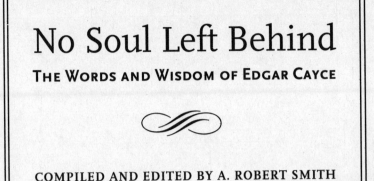

COMPILED AND EDITED BY A. ROBERT SMITH

CITADEL PRESS
KENSINGTON PUBLISHING CORP.
WWW.KENSINGTONBOOKS.COM

CITADEL PRESS BOOKS are published by

Kensington Publishing Corp.
850 Third Avenue
New York, NY 10022

Printed in the United States of America

ISBN 0-8065-2672-6

For Susan

Contents

Acknowledgments

MANY STUDENTS OF the Edgar Cayce readings contributed to my understanding of the philosophy that emerges from his vast body of work. First among them was Hugh Lynn Cayce, who devoted much time to tutoring me, which resulted in a biography, *About My Father's Business*. Secondly was saintly Gladys Davis Turner, Edgar Cayce's longtime secretary who facilitated my research in the Cayce archives, which resulted in my compiling and editing Cayce's memoirs, *Edgar Cayce: My Life As a Seer*. I am indebted to many writers whose work I encountered at *Venture Inward* magazine during my editorship, as well as the authors of Cayce books, among them Thomas Sugrue, Harmon H. Bro, Richard H. Drummond, Bruce MacArthur, William A. McGarey, Henry Reed, K. Paul Johnson, Violet Shelley, and Mark Thurston.

I am deeply indebted to Susan Lendvay, whose work in the readings research department of the Association for Research and Enlightenment and on the staff of *Venture Inward* has given her a rich understanding of the Cayce material. Her numerous valuable editorial suggestions and encouragement contributed immensely to the book and to its author.

I am grateful to Charles Thomas Cayce, president of the Edgar Cayce Foundation, for permission to quote extensively from the

Cayce readings; to Dan Campbell for his good suggestions; to Lisa Hagan, my agent at Paraview, for facilitating this publishing venture; and to Bob Shuman, the senior editor at Kensington, for peppering me with thoughtful questions and valuable suggestions that served this work well.

∽

A Message of Hope

LIFE IS AN endless, potentially joyful spiritual quest, says Edgar Cayce (1877–1945), America's most renowned seer. It is not confined to the often troubled span between birth and death as we time it, and least of all is it "nasty, brutish and short," as the English philosopher Thomas Hobbes insisted. But then Cayce is the consummate spiritual seeker while Hobbes a determined materialist who thought the soul to be merely mortal. Cayce believes the soul is immortal and that we are all embarked on a journey to become companions to God.

The focus of this book is Cayce's message of hope. His mystical visions provide a profoundly intriguing view of what life is all about. He offers us a high sense of purpose and a prescription for a fulfilling life in a time of mounting violence that crosses ethnic, religious, and international borders.

Cayce's philosophy is all the more remarkable because he made no effort to found a new sect. Indeed, his ecumenical system of belief is universal in scope, embracing all great faiths. As such, it drew him away from the fundamentalist Protestant religion of his roots.

A native of rural Christian County, Kentucky, Cayce was raised

by devout parents who read to him from the King James Version
of the Bible every evening, a practice he continued as an adult. By
"confessing faith in Christ" at age eleven, Cayce became a member of their Disciples of Christ church and a star pupil, reciting
Bible passages from memory in his father's Sunday school class.
By age fourteen he had "read the Bible through several times, understanding little; yet to my developing mind, this book seemed to
contain that something that my inner self craved."[1] He aspired to
become a preacher and sought out "ministers of all creeds and de-
nominations . . . seeking I knew not what." As a boy, he had a mystical experience that foreshadowed the direction of his life: an
angelic figure appeared to him after he had prayed for the ability
to help his fellow man, and it said, "Thy prayers are heard. You
will have your wish. . . . Help the sick, the afflicted."

Boyhood chums considered him strange—he frequently had
conversations with "the little folk" whom only he and his mother
saw in the woods and with his deceased grandfather, after seeing
the old gentleman drown in a pond. Their teasing made him determined to be as conventional as other boys. But it was not to be.
A poor speller in school, he discovered that by sleeping on his
textbook he could spell every word correctly when he awoke.
While he improved as a student with this gift, he was obliged to
quit school after the eighth grade and take a job to help support
the family (he had three young sisters). He farmed, clerked in a
bookstore, and sold insurance until he found a promising trade in
photography.

The mysterious loss of his voice as a young sales agent brought
on a major crisis, for doctors were unable to offer a cure. Sub-
mitting to hypnosis in a desperate effort to overcome his impedi-
ment, he fell into a trance, during which he described the cause of
his own condition and prescribed a treatment that restored his

---

1. Edgar Cayce, *My Life as a Seer*.

voice. As word spread of this remarkable feat, friends and neighbors with ailments that baffled physicians sought his aid. Although mystified by his own process, he submitted to hypnosis and proceeded to describe the cause and suggest a remedy, which frequently helped.[2]

Seeking no recognition or compensation for such healing assistance, he married a local girl, had three children, one dying in infancy, and supported his family as a studio photographer for fifteen years before he was persuaded to devote full time to serving as a medical clairvoyant. From that day, in 1923 at age forty-six, Cayce gave psychic readings on request, answering whatever questions were asked while he was in a trance and awaking with no recollection of what he had said. A secretary took it all down in shorthand and transcribed copies for his files and for the client. Many clients returned or recommended him to others, keeping him busy for nearly two decades.

The documentation his work generated—nearly 14,000 readings—did more than help the individuals who requested them, for Cayce's responses to wide-ranging metaphysical questions were often profoundly insightful and far beyond the narrow interests of the individual who inquired. From his lips poured complex explanations for the nature of life, the human soul and its eternal journey, the structure of the universe, the origin of humankind, our spiritual purpose, and much more. This outpouring of information has since inspired scores of books and many thousands of readers.

2. In one dramatic case, the parents of six-year-old Aime Dietrich, who suffered from convulsions, her mind a blank, gave a sworn statement that Cayce saved the child's life after a physician said her condition was terminal. Edgar found "congestion at the base of the brain" and suggested daily osteopathic treatments to soften the hardened membranes that had impeded circulation to the brain. "Her mind began to clear up about the eighth day," the Dietrichs reported, and "within three months she was in perfect health." When Aime turned sixteen, she came to visit the Cayces. "I don't think I have met many prettier girls," he said.

Cayce's devotion to healing led to his building a hospital at Virginia Beach, Virginia, and earned him the nickname "father of holistic healing."

More remarkable was the metaphysical cosmology that emerged from his work—an explanation of why we, the human race, are here and where we are going. Devout Christian though he was, Cayce produced a sophisticated ecumenical philosophy that surely would have got him expelled from the fundamentalist church of his youth. Indeed, even a mainline Presbyterian church in Virginia ousted him as a Bible teacher after learning that he subscribed to such unorthodox views as reincarnation and karma.

The heart of Cayce's philosophy is that all of us are on a spiritual quest, a far journey of the soul that takes us through numerous lives, into many realms of consciousness, with but one ultimate destiny: We are prodigals going home to God, to be welcomed by our Father. All of us.

Cayce's positive view contrasts sharply with the "rapture" doctrine preached by many Protestant fundamentalists. They portray God's domain as a gated community accessible only to a select number of the faithful who will soon be called home (raptured), leaving the rest of us behind. Embraced by evangelicals, the rapture theory has dubious parentage. The term *rapture*, from the Latin *rapere*, meaning "to be caught up" or "snatched," does not appear anywhere in the Bible, nor is it found in any early Christian writings. First espoused in 1830 by John Nelson Darby, the founder of the Plymouth Brethren sect in England, its only scriptural underpinning is found in I Thessalonians 4:16–17, which states that "the Lord Himself will descend from heaven with a shout, with the voice of an archangel, and with the trumpet of God. And the dead in Christ will rise first. Then we who are alive and remain shall be caught up together with them in the clouds to meet the Lord in the air. And thus we shall always be with the Lord."

Cyrus I. Scofield, an American publisher, seized on Darby's terminology and added "rapture" to the Scofield Reference Bible, misleading many readers to conclude that it was a biblical article of faith. Criticism of Scofield[3] did not diminish the popularity of his bible in twentieth-century America, notably among southern fundamentalist theologians.

Consequently, many Christians have been taught, as one commentator put it:

> that at some point in the near future, Jesus Christ will return and "snatch away" all Christians on the earth. Those who believe in Jesus will rise to meet Him in the air, and He will whisk them off to heaven for a $3^{1/2}$-to-seven-year Marriage Supper. In the meantime here on earth, untold destruction occurs when "born-again Christians" suddenly vanish while at the controls of cars, trucks, trains, airplanes, heavy equipment and the like. "Unsaved" relatives and friends will frantically and unsuccessfully search for their raptured loved ones. The media will provide 24-hour coverage of the mysterious disappearance of millions of people, speculating wildly on its cause—everything from a mass alien abduction to shifting dimensions and levels of consciousness. Does this sound like something our God would do?[4]

If Cayce ever heard of the rapture theory, he ignored it in his discourses and lectures. Instead, he consistently advanced his positive theology to those seeking his guidance. They asked not only about spiritual concerns but also everything imaginable about their personal lives and their business ventures.

3. Albertis Pieters in *A Candid Examination of the Scofield Bible* describes Scofield as "an intellectual charlatan, a fraud who pretends to knowledge which he does not possess, like a quack doctor."

4. Richard T. Ritenbaugh, in *Forerunner*, August 1996.

People came to him not because he and his work were highly publicized. A man of modest, almost shy, bearing, Cayce showed little talent for self-promotion. Indeed, the first national publicity his work received was near the end of his life, in 1943, when a biography, *There Is a River*, and an admiring article in a national magazine were published. Until then, save for a feature story in the *New York Times* and occasional articles in local newspapers in towns where he appeared, his reputation was built on word-of-mouth recommendations.

All of Cayce's words of wisdom have been preserved by the organization he founded in 1931, the Association for Research and Enlightenment, and are available in the reading room of the organization's world-class metaphysical library at Virginia Beach, as well as on CD-ROM and the World Wide Web. The concepts found in Edgar Cayce's nearly 14,000 clairvoyant readings have impressed scholars with their internal consistency. While he often struggled to describe multidimensional scenarios in terms understandable to those of us inhabiting a three-dimensional world (a glossary of unusual terms has been included to assist the reader), the concepts found in Cayce's readings have impressed scholars with their internal consistency. And the profound quality of much of the material has drawn people from all over the world to study Cayce's answers that remain relevant for people today.

The format of this book is the familiar interview style of a journalist asking questions that readers want answered. I formulated questions that many would ask Cayce today if he were still alive. His answers are those he gave in response to earlier inquiries, excerpted verbatim from his collection of readings and lightly edited for clarity. (Cayce often lapsed into the dated language of the King James Version, his favorite Bible text. Such pronouns as thee and thine, except when he quotes scripture, and a few colloquialisms have been modernized.) The essential wisdom of his ideas gives his statements timeless value.

Code numbers at the close of each quotation, assigned by his secretary to protect the privacy of the unidentified client, are included here for those who care to research the Cayce material beyond the scope of this book. Rewards are there for the digging.

A. Robert Smith
Virginia Beach, Virginia

No Soul Left Behind

CHAPTER 1

The Purpose of Life

WHY ARE WE here? All of us, the entire human race, past, present, and future?

For centuries, this challenging question has confronted philosophers, wise men, shamans, and people of all ages, of all races. For those who believe in a diety, there are a variety of answers that can be found in the creeds of the separate faiths. Agnostics, humanists, and others who reject the idea of a Supreme Being formulate their own explanation for human existence, as do the countless sects whose unorthodox beliefs fit no mold but their own. Too often, these diverse belief systems have led to bloodshed that violates most all creeds.

Edgar Cayce had a belief system that offers a hopeful alternative. It is rooted in the idea that the energizing spark of each one of us lies within our soul. It is there that we are made in the image of God. Therefore, the story of humankind is what happens to the soul, here on earth and far beyond the grave, on its grand quest through this world to realms beyond. His vision is more inclusive than exclusive. In this respect, Cayce serves as a unifying agent for people of all or of no faiths.

Humankind's purpose, our destiny, he explains, is to become nothing less than companions of God. How we are to live our lives to realize this noble objective is set forth in the interviews that follow.

I'm going to ask you about the great mysteries—about life and death and our destiny as individuals and as the human race, and whether we have a purpose here beyond ourselves. Let's start with some basics: What is responsible for life itself?

Life, or manifestation of that which is in motion, is receiving its impulses from a First Cause. 254-67

What do you mean by the First Cause?

That which has brought, is bringing, all life into being; or animation, or force, or power, or movement, or consciousness, on either the material plane, the mental plane, [or] the spiritual plane. Hence, it is the force that is called Lord, God, Jehovah, Yah, Abba, and the like. Hence the activity that is seen of any element in the material plane [such as the cycle of life seen in nature that stems from the planting of a seed] is a manifestation of that First Cause. 254-67

The First Cause, then, is the power of the Deity at work in the universe on all levels, which manifests or shows up as the sunshine that makes crops grow, or the creative energy of the mind of people, or the power of love and other spiritual values. But since millions of people on earth recognize and worship different deities with different names, is there really only one?

One Force. 254-67

By One Force, do you mean One God?

The Lord God is One. [There is but one deity.] Would that all souls could, would, comprehend that great sentence.... [It] is the motivating force in all who seek. Not in all who impel, but in all who seek to live, who seek to manifest, who seek to give expression of God's force or power. 2067-1

Man is ever in that field of being a channel, an emissary, for that [whom] he worships as his god. May that god ever be the Lord, God of Hosts—His name is One. 442-1

Why were we created in the first place?

God's desire for companionship and expression. 5749-14

Did God achieve that objective?

All souls in the beginning were one with the Father. The separation or turning away brought Evil. 262-56

When did the turning away happen—in the Garden of Eden?

Separation began before there appeared what we know as the earth, the heavens; or before space was manifested. 262-115

Why did God allow man this much freedom?

That he [man] may know himself, to be himself and yet one with the Father; separate, yet as Father, Son, and Holy Spirit are one, so the body, the mind, the soul of an entity may also be at-one with the First Cause. 815-7

This, I take it, is what is often called "the fall of man." Was this inevitable in the destiny of souls, or was it something that God did not want but did not prevent once He gave man free will?

He did not prevent it, once having given free will. For, He made the individual entities or souls in the beginning. For the beginnings of sin, of course, were in seeking expression of themselves outside of the plan or the way in which God had expressed same. Thus it was the individual, see? Having given free will, then, though having the foreknowledge, though being omnipotent and omnipresent, it is only when the soul that is a portion of God *chooses* that God knows the end thereof. 5749-14

If this was the "original sin," what was sinful about it?

All forms of sin or lessons may be implied in the word *selfishness.* 815-7

When God created souls, was it originally intended that souls remain in a spiritual form rather than take on a physical form in the earth?

The earth and its manifestations were only the expression of God and not necessarily as a place of tenancy for the souls of men.... The problem here is to reconcile the omniscience of God and His knowledge of all things with the free will of the soul and the soul's fall from grace. [We must accept that God knew what would happen by granting free will to all souls, and yet gave them the privilege of choosing their way in the world.] 5749-14

The experience of the human race has been terribly violent. Wars and lesser conflicts often begin between people of different religions who hate or can't accept the faith and practices of their neighbors. What do you say to people on either side in such conflicts, Arabs and Jews, or Protestants and Catholics?

The first lesson [you give them] for six months should be [the principle of] ONE—One—One—One; oneness of God, oneness of man's relation[ship to God], oneness of force, oneness of time, oneness of purpose, oneness in every effort—oneness, oneness. 900-429

You say oneness of purpose—that is, all people have the same purpose—but is there no room for individuality, each of us finding a personal purpose that is special for us?

Know that the Creative Energy called God may be as personal as an individual will allow...for the Spirit is in the image of the

Creative Forces [God] and seeks manifestation [expression]. It may take that personality, that personal activity that will be allowed by the individual itself; for we are co-laborers, co-creators with that energy we call God, that energy we call Universal Forces. While this may appear to be the Whole, if we will understand that "the Lord thy God is One" (Mark 12:29) and all power, all force emanates from that One Source, we will get an understanding of ourselves and our abilities [as we work in tandem with God, such as the gardener who cultivates the soil and plants the seeds so that God can transform them into a crop]. 391-4

So, what is the purpose that we all have?

The purposes, the import of the earthly sojourn of each soul, is to meet self, to overcome those weaknesses in self, and become more and more adaptable to spiritual truths [such as kindness and generosity] that are a part of each and every entity. For what gain is there in the experience of a soul [that seeks] to gain the world in fame, in fortune, in social relationships, and [manages] to lose self's own soul? For the soul is continuous. Life is in constructive forces [that serve humankind] or what you call God. 1362-1

In our society, it's hard to ignore the pressures for success in our chosen field and financial gains to support a family when so much emphasis is given these objectives. Many people would regard it as a big step backward if we abandoned such goals, as though we were reverting to a pastoral, more primitive society. I'm afraid it would cause much turmoil. What's our alternative?

Then to manifest patience, as well as persistence, to manifest brotherly love, to manifest long-suffering when there is known that the ideal and the purpose is right, is building that which is the schooling, the training, the qualifying for closer walks with God.

So until each soul, each entity, knows those closer walks, there must be, there are, turmoils in the experience of every soul; more and more mental, more and more material turmoils. But to be at peace, to be in harmony with constructive, creative forces, is to know Him that *is* the way, that is life; and in Him you live and move and have your being! 1362-1

That presupposes a faith or belief in God. What about the many people who claim to have no such faith or who simply believe in nature?

Each individual is, in reality, that manifestation of the individual's conception of the impelling force from within, whether it be termed or called God, nature, Universal Forces, natural powers, or what not. 900-234

In other words, it doesn't matter what you call the Power that gives life to all of us, and to animals and plants, even the nonbeliever can't deny the Deity's existence without denying life itself?

Life is, in all its manifestations in every animate force, [the] Creative Forces in action. 262-46

If the Creative Forces is another name for God, would it be fair to say that our individual creative efforts, such as the work of a poet or a painter, are a manifestation of the God force in these artists?

Life is creative and is the manifestation of that energy, that oneness, which may never be wholly discerned or discovered in materiality [if we don't allow time for such creative pursuits as the arts in our daily life]—and yet is the basis of all motivative forces and influences in the experiences of an individual. 2012-1

I see your point, that creativity is not limited to artists, for surely the birth of a child is the most profound creative act, or evidence of the Creative Forces. And life itself is creative. But what is life?

And what is life? God manifested in the material plane. For it is still in Him that we live and move and have our being (Acts 17:28). Thus life as a material manifestation is the expression of that Universal Force or Energy we call God. 3590-1 Life, as a whole, is a continuous thing emanating from power, energy, God-consciousness, ever. 1472-1 [Life is God] in power, in might, in the awareness of the strength needed to meet every problem day by day. 3161-1

I understand that it is everlasting and that it comes from God, but what is this energy that makes the difference between what is alive and what is lifeless?

All energy is electrical in its activity in a manifested form. 735-1 Life in its manifestations is vibration. Electricity is vibration. 1861-16 The vibratory force is the active principle [that] all radiates from. 195-54 All energy is electrical in its activity in a manifested form. 735-1 Electricity or vibration is that same energy, same power, you call God. Not that God is an electric light or an electric machine, but vibration that is creative is of the same energy as life itself. 2828-4 All power, all force, is a manifestation of what is termed the God-consciousness. 601-11

You say that God wants us to recognize our oneness, as though we were one big family. Is that our only purpose?

God seeks all to be one with Him. And as all things were made by Him, that which is the creative influence in every herb, every mineral, every vegetable, every individual activity, is that same force you call God—and [He] seeks expression! Even as when God said: "Let there be light," and there was light. 294-202

But aren't we often influenced, even directed, by other people or the special circumstances of our lives that we did not create, such as growing up in a crime-infested urban ghetto or in a friendly small town?

As to whether circumstances or environs [are] to rule an entity's being or experience, or will, depends then the most upon what the entity or soul sets as its standard of qualifications [such as high or low ideals] to meet or measure up to, within its own self; or as to how well self may be guided by its standard in making decisions in those directions. 590-1

Each entity is endowed with its choice. And the choice is the result of the application of self in relationships to its ideal—and finds manifestation in what individuals call habit, or subconscious activity. Yet it has its inception in that of choice. 830-2

There is that within self that is creative; and it, that creative force, cooperating with the Divine without, will lead to the choice of that which is life. And when the choice is made, then there may be a vision, astrologically and otherwise, of what end [purpose] thereof is. But each soul is given the birthright of the ability to choose—under any environment, circumstance, any experience. 1580-1

Young people are often led astray by poor choices in companions whom they may chance to meet in school, at work, or on the street. Or they may chance to be inspired by an uplifting person. Isn't that the chance we parents have to live with?

No association or experience is by chance, but is the outgrowth of a [universal] law, spiritual, mental, or material. 2753-2 There is nothing by chance. Friendships are only the renewing of former purposes, ideals. 2946-2 Each individual constantly meets [him- or her]self [we are drawn to situations that reflect our current values]. There are no coincidences, or accidents, that arise in the meeting of people or individuals. 2074-1 Nothing is by chance, but is . . . a pattern of . . . the choices made by the entity in its relationships to things, conditions, and . . . entities. 1825-1

But we meet so many people who influence us for better or for worse.

We meet few people by chance, but all are opportunities in one experience or another. We are due them or they are due us certain considerations. 3246-1

You mean there is some purpose to be served by each encounter?
Each entity enters a material experience for a purpose, not accidentally, not by chance. But life and its expressions are purposeful. 1792-2

I suppose we can learn something from every experience, and if our purpose is to become wiser, each encounter helps. But what is the purpose of life itself other than, as you said earlier, to acknowledge God?
The purposes for which each soul enters materiality are that it may become aware of its relationship to the Creative Forces or God. 1567-2 The purposes for each soul's experience in materiality [in the physical world] are that the Book of Remembrance may be opened that the soul may know its relationship to its Maker.[5]
1215-4

Wasn't that relationship defined by Jesus when he referred to God as the Father in Heaven? From that there seems a widespread belief, at least among His followers, that we are all God's children. But is our purpose simply to be worshipful children?
The entering of every soul is that it, the soul, may become more aware or conscious of the Divine within, that the soul-body may be purged [of material addictions or other destructive ways] that it may be a fit companion for the glory of the Creative Forces. 518-2

5. In an attempt to explain fourth-dimensional or spiritual experiences, such as this, Cayce often uses metaphors that employ three-dimensional objects that we might readily visualize, such as a book. Both sentences in this response suggest the same thing about the soul's purpose on earth, only one introduces the metaphor Book of Remembrances, meaning that the soul needs to remember its connection to God.

Beyond recognizing that God exists, if there is more to our purpose in this life, how does one fulfill it?

By the material manifestation of the things thought, said, [and] done, in relation to its fellow man. 1567-2

Little by little does one come to the understanding of the purpose for which they came into the earth. [Rising to meet that] purpose is of the making of the individual, plus that given in the beginning, and as souls seek[ing] the Father, in that companionship that one may have through communion with Him—and communion with Him means doing, not shutting self away from your brother, from your neighbor, even from yourself—rather applying self to duties material, mental, and spiritual, as is known. 99-8

The whole of the experience of an individual entity in a material plane is the coordinating and cooperation of [the] Creative Forces from without [the influence of God] to the divine [spark] within [the soul]. 1158-8

You speak of "communion with God" and "companionship" with Him as our destiny. How can we as fallible people ever hope to reach that lofty goal?

The purposes, the import of the earthly sojourn...is to meet self, to overcome those weaknesses in self, and [to] become more and more adaptable to the spiritual truths that are a part of each and every entity. 1362-1 Each sojourn or indwelling may be compared to what you have in your mental experience as a lesson, as a schooling for the purposes for which each soul-entity enters in earth experience; and why an entity under such environments came into that experience. Each study of each lesson then adds some phase of development for the soul. 1158-5

It seems an overwhelming task to overcome our own weaknesses, and yet you believe that life gives us a chance, an opportunity, to grow spiritually?

Through a physical body the soul has an opportunity to express the attainments developed in other spheres of consciousness [on the other side]. Life in the earth becomes an opportunity for paralleling, correlating, cooperating, [and] bringing into existence the effects of using all experience presented for the development of the soul. 262-50

How can we become wise enough to avoid bad choices?

Wisdom then is the divine love [of God] made manifest [expressed] in your daily conversation, your daily avocation, your daily acts as one to another [living a God-centered rather than a self-centered life]. *This* is Wisdom. This as you apply, this as you make known in your conversation, in your acts, will become more and more part and parcel of your *very* self. And though the earth may make for the calls [tempt us] for what is satisfying of the moment, the glorifying of self, the exalting of self—if you have the divine love you will find that in the application of your Knowledge, your Wisdom, the glory of the Christ is brought forth in your conversation, your daily life, your daily activity among your fellow men. Choose then this day *whom* you will serve: The Lord holy and righteous, or the self who is weak and unworthy of the love unless you show forth His Love as you have seen in your experiences [with those who love you], to your fellow man. 262-104

It is breathtaking to think that we might one day be companions with God.

Remember, you are corpuscles in the body of God, each with a duty, a function to perform if the world would be better for you having lived in it, and this is your purpose in the earth. 3481-2

In other words, our primary purpose is to learn to love our neighbor. And no matter what else we do with our creative gifts, we fulfill our purpose to the extent that we devote ourselves to the service of our brothers and sisters.

Know that the purpose for which each soul enters a material [earthly] experience is that it may be a light unto others. 641-6

⌇⌇

CHAPTER 2

Mind over Matter

A FAVORITE EXPRESSION of Cayce's is "Mind is the builder." It is his way of explaining that the way we use or focus our mind has lasting consequences. For thoughts are lasting things, not perishables that are easily dismissed. What we think eventually forms attitudes and leads to our behavior. In a word, what the mind dwells on shapes who and what we are, whether we are focused on gaining power, fame, and fortune or are more intent on serving our fellow humans.

The mind, he explains, is immortal and perpetuates the thought patterns that we have built. We can override our baser thoughts by meditating on our higher ideals and choosing the fruits of the spirit over the pleasures of materiality.

The major distinction you make between the physical body and the soul, or soul-body, is that the one is temporary and the other permanent or eternal. But what about the mind? Is it purely physical or is it part of our eternal spirit that survives after the death of the body?

This [answer], to be sure, will be as a portion or a lesson in itself, including Mind in relation to the varied attributes of the physical, the mental, and the spiritual bodies. Mind in itself, then, is both material *and* spiritual. That which finds itself expressed or manifested in material things is of the physical, for matter is an expression of spirit in motion to such a degree as to give the expressions in materiality.

That which is expressed or manifested in spirit, without taking body or form, is of the spirit; yet may be manifested in [a mystical] experience of an individual [such as a communication from a deceased loved one]... the ideal must have its inception in, from, and with that which is an unseen force, or in what we may worship as a God. 262-78

What do you mean by the ideal?

Ideals are principles acted upon by your mind. 2533-6

What we are—in any given experience or time—is the combined result of what we have done about the ideals that we have set. 1549-1

The goal of many people is to become wealthy or famous—would that be their ideal?

An ideal cannot, should not, will not, be what is man-made, but must be of the spiritual nature—that has its foundation in Truth, in God. 262-11

You mean it is up to us to select spiritual ideals?

[An ideal] may be the continued reaching out [to others] of an individual, whether applied to the physical life, the mental life, or the spiritual life.[6] 262-11

These experiences—whether physical, mental, or spiritual— [that] may be judged or from which conclusions may be drawn

6. As a practical matter, Cayce suggested compiling a list of ideals in three areas: physical, such as getting sufficient exercise; mental, reading or traveling to expand our understanding of the life of other people; and spiritual, such as offering daily prayers and assisting those less fortunate.

[about how we are living our lives]. Otherwise we are measuring ourselves *by* ourselves, and this becomes unwise. 954-5

There is one ideal—that which manifests in the earth in the Christ-Jesus. That should be every entity's ideal—physically, mentally, and materially—for, He is the light, He is the way, He is the truth. 2533-7

Since ideals are acted on by the mind, do they help shape the development of the mind, or is the mind like a muscle that lifts or bends as need be but is buried and forgotten when our physical body dies?

Know that life and mind are eternal.... For as the mind and the life are a part of the eternal consciousness, then only constructive thought and activity may *make* for the better physical as well as *mental* development!

The body is physical, mental, and spiritual. These are one, and they manifest in materiality through the activities of the body-mental and the body-physical. But if the body is fed only upon that which is temporal in its concept, in its activity [such as gaining wealth], then it must of itself become a burden sooner or later. For only that which is Good, that which is constructive, that which is true, that which is spiritual, can live—or *does* live *on* and *on!* 1691-1

What is the spiritual role that the mind plays?

Mind, then, may function without a form or body. Hence we will give, at this particular portion of this [answer]... an outline of those conditions, experiences, or manifestations that may be had by the mind irrespective of the body: In the beginning God created the heavens and the earth. How? The *mind* of God *moved*, and matter, form, came into being.

Mind, then, in God, the Father, is the builder. How much more, then, would or should Mind be the builder in the experience of those that have put on Christ or God, in Him, in His coming into the earth? For as He has given, "Let that mind be in you which was in the Christ, who thought it not robbery to make Himself equal with God," but living in materiality in the earth, in matter, as a body; but with the Mind, with the thought, with the manifestations of a Creative Force all together. 262-78

Does the Mind influence our soul growth?

What you think, what you put your Mind to work upon, to live upon, to feed upon, to live with, to abide with, to associate with in the mind, that your soul-body becomes! That is the law. That is the Destiny. That *is* as from the beginning, that each thought of the Creator bore within itself its own fruit as from the beginning. 262-78

It's a pretty horrible concept, that our thoughts just accumulate and are never deleted? Why is that?

How does matter, how does the seed of the oak or of the grass or of the flower or of the tree or of the animal or of the man, find within itself that which impels, propagates the species, the activative [life] force that moves on in its realm of activity in whatever sphere [any of the realms of the universe] it may find itself, giving expressions of that first thought of the Creative Forces? That is its Destiny, which the Easterners say was set in the first. But, as you see, this is only half a truth. For if the Mind dwells upon the spiritual things, then it follows that it becomes what it has dwelt upon, what it has lived upon, what it has made itself a portion of. But if the Mind dwells upon self-indulgence, self-aggrandizement, self-exaltation, selfishness in any of its forms, in any of its variations, then it has set itself at variance to that First Cause; and we have that entered in as from the beginning, that of making the will through the Mind at variance to [the] Creative Forces before it has come into matter, into the movements in matter that we know as physical, material, as those things that are of the earth—earthy.

Yet we find the law, the same law, applying throughout the universe. For what enabled man, or a mind, to first comprehend? . . .

So as you contemplate, as you meditate, as you look upon the Mind, know the Mind has many windows. And as you look out of your inner self, know where you are looking, you are seeking. What is your ideal? What would you have your mind-body to become? For that on which it feeds it becomes, either by thought, by assimilation, by activity... by atomic influence, by the very influence of its activity in *whatever sphere* that activity may be within. And in the material mind it is the same.

Hence, as turning then to the physical Mind: This becomes necessary... for the application of the Mind, for the preparations for its activity in the material world. Yet these become so intermingled, so much a portion in the body and out of the body, that often one becomes confused as to what is of spiritual import and what is of the material or the necessities of same. Yet you are seeking in this to know what is the Destiny of the Mind. What has been set? Where is your Destiny? It is in what one does about what one knows that one becomes in oneself. For it is oneself from one's portion or activity of that first movement of Mind from the spiritual aspect or from the material aspect. 262-78

Does the mind dictate to the soul, or the soul dictate to the mind?

This depends upon the approach the individual makes to same. The Mind is both of the soul and of the material things. To clarify this, let's give an example: A body-mind, through its own self, raises in the mental power that which is for the satisfying of the desires of the flesh, that may find their manifestations in power, in fame, in fortune, in the place of this, that or the other seen before men. This is applying the mind in the earthly realm, see? Then there may be the applying of the mind, *holding* to that attitude of "Lord, use me as thou sees fit," you see; seeking only for the material manifestations which may hold that in perfect accord with what may be manifested through physical or material activities of the individual. Then the psychic forces [soul] are from those meetings within, not the aggrandizement of self or self's attributes towards the material of the physical standards, but towards what is to be the activity of the spirit of truth [and such other fruits of the spirit as love and kindness] in Him. 531-4

So, whatever we think is what we become at the level of our soul?

The experiences of the entity in the earth become an influence...just as it is true that what you think you become, just as what you consume for the physical [whether it be a balanced nutritious diet or a careless indulgence, say, in sweets or alcohol] produces such experience in your physical and mental life as related to the ideals, whether known or still latent. 1895-1

But if you are well-grounded in those tenets, in that truth which has been presented here for your own consideration, for your own application in your individual experience, then you may set many a mind aright; and let, and have, and see their lives becoming more and more constructive in their daily experience, with their fellow man and in relationships with those they meet day by day.

For what is applicable to one is in the same relationship to self. For when those activities become such that the Mind of the individual, of the soul, finds itself expressing itself in the physical, in the mental, the body will take on what? Immortality! In the earth? Yes; reflecting same that it may bring what is as the tree of life in the garden, that its leaves are for the healings of the nations; that are the leaves that may fall from your lips, from your activities to your fellow man, in whatever sphere or realm of activity. Why? Because of your own self, because you are grounded in the water of life itself, as you grow upon those inflowings and outflowings of the spirit of Him that gave, "Let that mind be in you which is in me, that as I abide in the Father and you abide in me, we may be one with Him," which is the Destiny of those that love His coming. 262-78

Can't we purge our minds or guard against the negative thoughts that tend to crowd in during the day?

In whatever manner, that your own consciousness is a cleansing of the body and of the mind, that you may present yourself *clean* before yourself and before your God, *do [it]*! Whether washing of the body with water, purging of same with oils, or surrounding same with music or incense. But do what your *consciousness* directs you! Not questioning [it]! For he that doubts [his conscience] has already built his barrier [to finding God's way]!

Then, meditate upon that which is your highest ideal within yourself, raise the vibrations from your lower self, your lower consciousness through the centers of your body to the temple of the mind, the brain, the you that is single in purpose; or to the glandular forces of the body as the single you. Then, listen—listen! For it is not in the storm, not in the noise, but the still small voice that rises within.

And let your query ever be: Here am I, oh God, use me—send me! Do with me as thou seest! Not my will, but thine, oh God, be done in and through me.

These are the manners [by which we should live]. Not that the things of the material mind are to be neglected, but remember this: It is the foolishness of God that is the wisdom of man. It is the wisdom of man misapplied that is the foolishness to God. 826-11

Hence as these records or interpretations are given, it is the desire to give the entity a premise, an ideal, that it may answer to that search from within as to how to make this experience more worthwhile in this particular sojourn.

Know that man, as has been expressed, was given dominion over all, and in the understanding of same may use all of the laws pertaining to same for his benefit. 1895-1

CHAPTER 3

⌇

Relationships: Love and Sex

CAYCE IS NOT mystified by the age-old human condition that relationships are the greatest concern of the human race. We suffer conflicts in love or family relationships, on the job, or getting on with friends and neighbors. We try to avoid wars to enjoy the blessings of peace, too often in vain. Cayce observes that we have a common failing: We don't know how, or don't care to, love one another. He means love with a spiritual dimension, not just romance. The same advice applies to sex: Physical intimacy without love is inadvisable. Marriage, based on love and mutual respect, is ideal, but successful variations in this traditional pattern are possible within a framework of true giving.

What can we do to improve our relationships, at home, at work, wherever?

Let the law of the Lord[7] be your guide day by day, that there may be in all of your relationships no regrets. 1005-12

---

7. Cayce frequently used the expression "law of the Lord," or "God's law," or simply law to mean a commandment, such as the Ten Commandments received by Moses.

What do you mean by the law of the Lord?

Truth is the unalterable, unchangeable law, ever. What is Truth? Law! What is Law? Love. [The first spiritual law is to love God and your neighbor as yourself.] What is Love? God. What is God? Law and Love. These are the cycle of truth itself. And wherever you are, in whatever clime, its ever the same. 3574-2

Most of us have difficulty being completely truthful all the time—we often excuse "little white lies." How can we observe the truth more consistently?

Cultivate it in your mind and it will alter the results in your physical being. Yes, you will have much to live for. For everyone will be your friend, as you have something to give to everyone. Not what brings fault or brings want, and indeed makes an individual poor, but what is a blessing to the mind and to the soul, by giving grains of truth that take from no one, but add something to everyone.

Know in what spirit you do everything, and that in the spirit of truth—and find it in your own self. For there it may indeed be put to work for Good. 3574-2

In other words, be truthful, and it will pay off in our various relationships. You mention the law of love—what is the essential quality of the love you speak of?

Giving. As is given in this injunction, "Love thy neighbor as thyself." As is given in the injunction, "Love the Lord thy God with all thine heart, thine soul, and thine body." 3744-5

What do you mean when you say that "giving" is the essence of love? What should we give?

Brotherly love, kindness, mercy, patience, love, long-suffering [enduring provocation or injury long and patiently]. Against such [virtues] there is no law, for they are the law of love. 262-50

Many good souls show these wonderful traits, at least occasionally. But since we are innately self-centered—it is how we are born—how can we change?

He that contributes only to his own welfare soon finds little to work for. 3478-2

And yet it often takes years, even a lifetime, to overcome naturally selfish habits and work for the greater welfare of others, doesn't it?

True, an individual, a soul, must become less and less of self—or thoughts of self.... These then are conditions in all the relationships, in the home, in the associations, in the domestic relations, in the activities. Whatever your choice is, let these be ever with an eye single to service to that living influence of being a better, a greater channel of blessings to someone. Not of self choosing an easier way; not of self attempting to escape what is necessary for your own understanding, your own soul development; but rather ever, "Your will, O Lord, be done in and through me—use me as You see I have need of, that I may be a living example of your love, of your guidance in this material experience." 845-4

If we are more giving, can we expect others to be more friendly or less antagonistic toward us?

The gift, the giving, with hope of reward or pay is direct opposition of the law of love. Remember there is no greater than the injunction, "God so loved His creation, or the world, as to give His only begotten son, for their redemption." Through that love, as man makes it manifest in his own heart and life, does it reach [fulfill] that law, and in compliance of a Law, the law becomes a part of the individual. What is the law of love? Giving in action, without the force felt, expressed, manifested, shown, desired, or reward for what [is] given. Not that the law of love does away with other laws, but makes the law of recompense, the law of faith, the law of divine, with the law of earth forces, if you please, effective, not defective.

So we have Love is Law, Law is Love. God is Love. Love is God. In that [love] we see the law manifested, not the law itself.... Now, if we, as individuals, upon the earth plane, have all of the other elementary forces that make to the bettering of life, and have not love we are nothing—nothing. "Though one may have the gift of prophecy, so as to give great understanding, even of the graces in hope, in charity, in faith, and has not the law of love in their heart, soul, mind and though they give their body to give itself for manifesting even these graces, and has not love they are nothing." In many, many ways may the manifestations of the law of love be shown, but without the greater love, even as the Father gives, even as the soul gives, there is no understanding, and no compliance of the forces that make our later law effective. 3744-5

Psychologists refer to some people as codependent when they knock themselves out trying to help others to the exclusion of taking care of themselves—the opposite of self-centeredness. Is there a danger in that?

He that contributes only to the welfare of others soon finds too much of others and has lost the appreciation of self, or of its ideals. 3478-2

So, we have to strike a balance between giving to others and to ourself in order to love our neighbor as ourself. What about God's love?

What is Love Divine? That the Father and the Son and the Holy Spirit may direct you, does direct you, will direct you in every thought, in every act! And judge not others, condemn not others. This is not love divine, neither is it wisdom. For it builds barriers, it destroys, it undermines the life of self first and then in the hearts and minds and experiences of others brings sorrow, disappointments, and those things that make the hearts of men afraid. 262-104

*Not everyone has conflicted relationships, and some couples are so har-
monious and so strongly attracted to one another that they believe they
are soul mates. Are there really soul mates—and if so, what distin-
guishes them from ordinary relationships?*

Those of any sect or group where there is the answering of one
to another, [such] as would be [in carpentry] the tongue to the
groove, the tenon to the mortise; or in any such where they are a
complement one of another—that is what is meant by "soul
mate." Not from physical attraction, but from the mental and spiritual help [each offers the other, such as a physician might have
with his or her nurse]. 1556-2

*If we are all one, why don't we experience the same harmony with
everyone?*

Do not misinterpret, but knowing that all are one—yet there
are those divisions that make for a closer union, when there are
the proper relationships brought about. As an illustration, in this:
In the material world we find there is in the mineral kingdom
those elements that are of the nature as to form a closer union one
with another and make compounds[8] ... that act more in unison
with, or against, other forms of activity in the experience in the
earth's environ. 364-7

*Was it God's intent when He created souls that we fulfill our purpose as
individuals or through partnerships?*

The gift of God to man is an individual soul that may be one
with Him, and that may know itself to be one with Him and yet
individual in itself, with the attributes of the whole, yet not the
whole. 262-11

For he, man, has been made just a little lower than the angels;
with all the abilities to become one with Him! Not the whole, nor

---

8. Bronze alloy is an example, a compound of copper and tin.

yet lost in the individuality of the whole, but becoming more and more personal in all of its consciousness of the application of the individuality of the Creative Forces, thus more and more at-onement with Him—yet conscious of being himself. 2172-1

If the Bible is right, was Adam not content with individuality but wanted companionship?

Adam, as given [in Genesis], discerns that from himself, not from the beasts about him, could be drawn—was drawn that which made for the propagation of beings in the flesh, that made for that companionship as seen by creation in the material worlds about same. 364-5

You've said that God created souls that they might become His companions. Was Adam's wish—and is our wish—for companionship a reflection in the human soul of God's wish?

The story [of Adam and Eve] is one and the same. The apple, as "apple of the eye," [symbolizes] the desire of that companionship innate in that created [soul], as innate in the Creator, that brought companionship into creation itself. 364-5

Am I right to believe that God did not intend for man to be alone, and that even though we stumble through difficult relationships, often feeling as much pain as pleasure, we can learn valuable lessons that aren't available to loners—how to give love to another person, for one?

In this...as is held by many who have reached especially to that understanding of how necessary, then, becomes the proper mating of those souls that may be then answers one to another of what may bring, through that association, that companionship, into being, what may be the more helpful, more sustaining, more well-rounded life or experience of those that are a portion one of the other. 364-7

You have said that "thoughts are things" that cannot be dismissed. Are we held accountable for our thoughts about others?

Man is often guilty of immoral action in the mind, for, as was given by the Master that it has been written that man shall not commit adultery, "Yea, I say unto thee that he that looketh on a woman to lust after her has committed adultery already." Here we see the change in the application of the lesson respecting morality as was governed under the law, taking the actual fact in action to produce that man called guilty of, while in the law of love we find that the greater sin may be in the desire of flesh towards the gratification of fleshly lusts; and in that manner the moralist may be the greater immoral person, and in such action the results are the fruit of what is gained through that activity of the body-mind, the body-consciousness, the inner consciousness of an individual. Keep your heart pure, that the issues therefrom may be in keeping wholly to that of the body-mind and body activity. 900-347

So, we are held accountable for impure thoughts, even when they don't lead to improper behavior?

The actions of the individual toward that of another individual known to the entity are as the truths as given, that thoughts are deeds and become crimes or miracles in the application; and whether meted in material plane or measured in the spiritual plane are as one, see? 900-331

I thought we had a free ride on our private thoughts, as long as we behaved appropriately. St. Paul urged people to behave in a moral manner to realize the fruits of the spirit. Is that a prescription for us today?

Rather, the understanding of those lessons given by Paul, yet many wrestle with them to their own undoing—meaning that it is not all to be learned in the material sense. Rather, be in that manner as learned in the spiritual sense, with that understanding that to do Good is to live Good, and not [just] to appear Good. Be

Good—not just appear Good. To live love is to be love. To be one with the Father is to be equal with the Father. And as the understanding of the entity is gained in the application of truths gained, the consciousness [awareness] of truth is apparent—for, as has been given, to love is to live love—not the answer of desire or of amorous affection, but is all in one—for love is law, law is love. 900-331

Conflict arises in some marriages over the roles of each partner, especially when women become "liberated" from domestic duties to seek their own careers. What is your perspective on this?

The greatest career of any wife is creating, making, building a home that is of such a nature, so attractive that it becomes what is intended and purposed to be. 1579-1

But many women today prefer to devote more time and energy to their careers.

There may be chosen the career or there may be chosen the home. Whichever one will make you happier than the other, then choose that! As has been given from the first, know the desire of the heart—know what is the ideal—then choose and work towards that! 349-8

Your wife worked with you for many years, first in your photo studio, and then in conducting your readings. And I gather it was your idea.

The greatest career of any individual, which is permitted to the wife, is to build the home in such a way and manner as to make it a retreat, as a place where all of those activities are such that it fills the longing that is in the heart and soul of each and every individual who has taken a mate for such.

As to whether this can be combined with a career or not is dependent upon the application of self in the directions of its abilities; for it may be used as same. But do not let other associations or affiliations make it rather as a place to hang the hat or to rest. Build a home! 1579-1

Your son, Hugh Lynn Cayce, told me that his mother did just that, not only working with you but managing the domestic side of your family life. What other advice do you have for couples to achieve a harmonious and happy relationship?

Analyze what are your purposes and desires. Analyze what the purposes and desires were that brought you and your spouse together. If they were for a gratifying only of physical, or for the desires of a physical nature, that's all there will ever be then!

But go deeper; and if there is the attempt, and the real attempt, and the analyzing of the purposes of each, they can be understood and each become a strength, as a stay [support] one for the other. For that which prompted the very activity of being brought into the relationship was from the spiritual import, while having the physical, the mental, as well as [the] spiritual aspects. Build them into a creative, constructive, and spiritual force. 1579-1

Is seeking fame or fortune contrary to a spiritual life?

The price must be paid! There is no such thing as receiving without giving; for he that would have life must give life, he that would have joy must make joy in the lives of others, he that would have peace and harmony must create and make peace in self and in relationships with others. This is the law, for like begets like; and you do not gather olives from thistles, neither apples from bramble bushes, neither do you find love in hate. 349-17

Do we always have to choose, forsaking one choice for the other?

As to the choices, these must ever be in self. For, if free will or the desire (which is an attribute or an expression of will) were taken from man, or from the human soul, it would then become rather the automaton, rather the animal, or rather the spirit of animal activity in a material world; hence not of itself. Rather, when the activity is not of self, let it be not in materiality but in spirituality—and the expressions thereof in self's activities. 349-17

Many careers offer creative work that requires the person to be giving. Is this less valuable or honorable than homemaking?

If the desire of the heart, of the mind, is such as to build rather a career, that is for the gratification of those interests that are creative within themselves to bring certain characters of activity. But the very purposes that have been given you, that you would find in the very activity that which must give of the very body itself in carnal desire to build for such experiences, should make for the knowledge within self that in such a field that has come to mean this in the lives of others you cannot gather Good from Evil. You cannot do Evil that Good may come of same. You cannot submerge yourself that these can be the better.... For, what you sow you must reap. Have you sown in dishonor, have you sown in making your conscience subjugated to that which tells within self that this is not the way; then you must reap that which comes....

Success may be made in the activities on the stage or in the cinema, for there is continuing to be sought the new faces, the new types, for feeding the bodies of same to what? Indulgencies of one character, nature, or another! And while they may build and may draw interest within self that will satisfy an ambition, as we have given, ambition—unless it is tested in God's crucible—is of itself sin. Not that one should not be ambitious, no—but rather ambitious that God should be the guide and not self, or man. 349-17

When you have counseled people who wanted careers in the entertainment world, what did you say to them?

Then be an actress! Self and soul is the price! The body and soul is the price!

If you have chosen with yourself that you are ready to pay the price, you may rise to heights that few have scaled—but what if you gain the whole world in fame, fortune, position, even in power, and lose your own soul? 349-17

When conflicts occur within an intimate relationship, what is the secret of reconciliation?

It must begin first within self. Is there the desire on the part of self for such [reconciliation with the partner]? It is needed in yourself, because there are mental conditions, there are those associations that will hinder one's abilities to serve in other directions. Yes, if there is even the offering to forgive and forget, don't forgive and say "I'll remember it—I forgive you but I'll keep on remembering it." If you do, you'd better not try it! 5001-1

What can a man do to enjoy a happier and more harmonious marriage?

Act toward the wife, or his own activities, as he would like her or others to act toward him. Ask no more than you give. Demand no more than you allowed, or allow, to be demanded of you. Marriage, such an association, is a oneness of purpose. Unless there is the oneness of purpose, there can be no harmony. This can be accomplished, not of self alone. For remember, if you made a mighty mess in the experience before this, you suffered for it! Better make it up now or it'll be ten times worse the next time! 5001-1

It was more difficult to get a divorce in your day, before the adoption of "no-fault" divorce statutes. Do you think marriage should be forever?

When periods come in the experience of each soul that the associations are unbearable, as to become hindrances to their keeping their own ideal, then to awaken or to attune or to change, or to alter those associations becomes necessary. 1192-7

By alter their associations, do you mean separation or divorce?

Each should look into their own consciousnesses. Each should answer that which has been given as from old, "Today is set before thee Good and Evil, life and death."

These should be then counseled, not in fury, not grudgingly, not in hate nor in condemnation. For what we condemn in another we must meet in our own selves. For God is not mocked, and whatever a soul sows, that it must reap. That our ideals are not of the same is apparent to all; and while man may often look upon the outward appearance, God judges from the heart and from the purpose of every act, every word, every desire. 1192-7

Do you favor marital counseling when conflicts burden a relationship?

We would counsel together, as to the obligations, the duties, the disturbances, the hopes, the disappointments, the shadows— the brightness that has been should be held rather than the darkness that may bring even greater fear and doubt.

But in prayerful meditation counsel within self as to the approach: not stern, not just forgiving without a purposefulness, but in love, in simplicity, state, give your own feelings, your own desires, and see if they coordinate or cooperate with the purposes and desires that may be stated by [your partner].

If these are so far [apart] then that they may not be drawn sufficiently together for a purposeful life, [it is] well that changes be [made]. If the fear is being overshadowed by a determination to put the trust rather in material things, then only in prayer, only in love may there be brought to the consciousness of the entity that great love, that forbearance, that patience that is the basis of a great soul. 1192-7

Suppose your partner isn't willing to make changes to improve the relationship?

Condemn not that which is your brother's mote, or that which is in your brother's eye, lest there comes that day when you meet your own conscience, your own self. But in love, in patience, reason together. For your spouse's soul is great in the eyes of his Maker, for his love and his patience and his labors in the experiences in the earth are far, far afield from that seen in the acts and the deeds of today. Yet you may indeed hold, you may indeed at least offer the opportunity and the way for that awakening—and not from without may it come, but from within!

The best, as has been indicated, is in the possible awakening of or in your companion the abilities, the goodness, the nobleness that is indeed there—if it will but be aroused to those possibilities, those opportunities that are before him. These make for the greater security. If these fail, then trust in Him only—that in the Giver of all Good and perfect gifts. And in your daily conversation, in your daily acts with your fellow man, show forth by same where your trust, your faith has been put. For to claim or to act in one way and then to think or feel or say unkind things makes all null and void.

For if you would have love, be lovely. If you would have friends, be friendly. If you would have faith, show it. And as is the law, it will come back to you! This is the greater security for self, for son. For you are indeed God's children, and he has given and does give His love each day. Then show in your love, in your patience, even in your long-suffering, the appreciations of that love. For He does not fail those that trust in Him. For He has given from the beginning, "Be my child and I will be your God." 1192-7

People sometimes make major changes—move to another town or take another job—in hopes of improving their relationships. Is this advisable?

Rather, as has been given, it must be an arousing within that will change the surroundings, the environs, the outlook, the desires, the hopes. For it is fear of the present and the future, and the attempts to produce within the very activities that which would justify self in things said and done. 1192-7

How should couples decide when to give or to take?

[They] should realize that there are obligations and duties that each one owes to those for whom they have been responsible, for the development and training of lives, of life itself and the part it has to play in contributing to the better welfare of those minds and bodies. Then, though there may be conditions not conducive to the better fulfilling of personal desires, these should be foregone in the face of obligations to others.

And, as has been given, the law of the Lord is perfect. You cannot escape your responsibility, and you cannot make peace with others until you find peace within your own consciousness. These, then, should be the manners in which judgments should be drawn.

Each should study and know that this union of activity has been and is chosen by [your]self. Then remain true to the promises, to the obligations, and be not in self overcome with those things which if embraced will cause continual stumblings.... Then, so live within your own self that the consciousness of self replies back. Not that you've got [an] advantage over the other fellow, not that you would become pessimistic, but rather: "Lord, here am I. Use me. Let my life, my purposes in same, through the power in those influences with which I have worshiped and do worship, bring that ability in me; to choose to do that which is right at all times, irrespective of the cost or expense to myself—mentally or materially." For indeed it is true that the flesh is often weak, yet the spirit is willing. 1449-2

How can we get into the mind of the Creator and do what He would have us do?

Is your purpose, is your desire one with Him? These be your

tests.... In manifesting relationships with your fellow man [do you show] the fruits of the spirit? Have you grown more tolerant? Have you grown more patient? Have you shown more brotherly love? Have you given of yourself, denying yourself that they who have lost hope, they who are wandering, they who are discouraged might be encouraged, find hope?

Then you know you are growing in grace, in knowledge, in understanding of your purposes in the earth.

Have you grown to be so they who meet you day by day take thought that you have in your mental self walked with your Maker?

These you answer from within yourself. These you know, these you understand. Follow in the way that leads to everlasting love, for He is love. 816-10

Does being smarter help us get along with other people better?

Gain first that knowledge within self of its, the entity's at-onement with the Creative Forces that manifest and have manifested themselves among men; in the applications of the Law of One; that is: God is, and is one!

Hence all force, all power comes from that as an influence and force; man's application making it as an at-onement with or as a directing of it for self's own indulgence, glorification, or satisfaction.

Love, then, divine as was manifested in Jesus of Nazareth, must be the rule, the measuring stick, the rod, by which you shall judge your motives, your impulses, your associations. For without Him there is not anything made that is made—to endure.

Man may produce the stumbling-stones; God alone—in the heart of man—may make them stepping-stones! Love the Lord, keep His ways, manifest them in every walk of life. Let others do as they may, but as for you and your house, love, obey the living God! 1497-1

What are the keys to a successful intimate relationship?

Much, to be sure, has to be worked out; in their application of not indulgences, not dependencies, not laudation one towards another, but in patience, in tolerance, in love that is truly manifest between those that would show forth in their every relation these attributes in their combined effort toward their fellow man. Then, these used or applied in these ways and manners will make for a union that is holy, that is acceptable to Him.

Each soul has its share not only of responsibility one toward the other, but of dependency one upon the other. Let both ever strive in their relationships, then, to become more and more a complement one to the other. And in this manner may there come to each a life experience more and more worthwhile. Then more and more may the beauties of purposefulness, of righteousness, of patience, of love, grow to be more beauteous, more worthwhile in the experience of each.

There may arise—and, as we find, there will arise—some experiences that for the moment will make it appear that this was not the more propitious time; yet we find that those experiences which are to arise in the life of each will be made much better, much more worth while, if this union of purpose is accomplished in this present season.

Periods will arise when due consideration must be given to each, in your outlook, your obligations, your purposes; but let each know that this union of purpose must be ever in the light of what your Father, your God, your Savior, would have you do! Let the ideals ever be set, then, in Him. Then those periods of turmoil, of fears and doubts on the part of each, will become stepping-stones for a greater and greater love, a greater expression of His love.

Let both find their own interpretations, but let both apply those interpretations in the light of His love; then they will be found to be one.

In your applications of the whole of purposefulness, let it

never be just for self. Consider others, even as He. Yet in the applications, let them be as one. Know that it is a fifty-fifty union. One should not always be forgiving and the other forgiven! But let both in their own selves look to and for that which will make the experience, the association, and the union of purpose, more and more as an exemplification of His Spirit, His love, His blessings upon all that you do; so living, so acting, that you may make this as the real standard, the real experience, the real beginning of each becoming more and more, more and more worthwhile.

Let both assume the obligations; not merely as obligations, not as duties alone, but as loving opportunities for each to be that helpmate to the other which will make a life of beauty, of joy; not only to selves but to others also. 849-12

You've talked about love as a prime mover in human relations, but you did not mention sex. What is its place in our lives?

There is no soul but what the sex life becomes the greater influence in life. 911-2

Why is that?

The material things (or those in a three-dimensional world) are the shadow or the reflection of those in the spiritual life. Then, as God or the Creative Influence is the source of all things, the second law in spiritual life, in mental life, in material life, is preservation of self and the continuation of likes, or propagation, in sexual intercourse or life. Hence, in their very basic forces, the relations in sexual life should be the outcome [in order to propagate life]—not the purpose of, but the outcome of the answering of soul to soul in their associations and relations. And the act, or the associations in this nature, should be the result.

Hence these questions should be often weighed well, remembering that God, or Love (for it is One), looks on the heart rather than the outward appearances....

For, in the understandings, know that Love and God are One; that relations in the sexual life are the manifestations in the mental attributes of each as to an expression of what becomes manifested in the experience of each so concerned. For, unless such associations become on such a basis, they become vile in the experience of those that join in such relations. 272-7

Sex obviously is the most profoundly creative act since Creation; but does our sexuality also influence other forms of creativity, such as the arts—music, writing, painting, and many others?

As sex is that channel through which creation in the material world brings forth that which is of creating itself, so are the organs of same—the centers through which all creative energies—whether mental or spiritual—find their inception in a material world for an expression. As has been given, when this force in sex is raised, or rated, in its inception through the mental forces [thoughts or desires] of the body, this finds expression in that of giving the love influence in the life or lives of the individual, as well as what may be brought into being as a gratification of a physical desire. [Sexual desire, in short, is the trigger for perpetuating the human specie, and it fosters love relationships that also gratify physical desires.] 911-2

Does sexual incompatibility hamper creativity?

Incompatibility that is between two individuals as given here, is that which makes for the inability for any creative forces to become compatible between the individuals. . . . Not always in gratification in the physical act, but rather what finds expression in the creative forces and creative abilities of the body itself. 911-2

The Bible story of the Garden of Eden suggests that God's children messed up in some way. Was this where our problem with sex began?

Adam and Eve, the knowledge of their position, or what is known in the material world today as desires and physical bodily charms, the understanding of sex, sex relationships, came into the [human] experience. With these [two individuals] came the natural fear of what had been forbidden, what they know themselves to be a part of but not of that partook of earthly, or the desires in the manner as were about them, in what had been their heritage. . . .

Hence we have found throughout the ages, so often the times when conception of truth became rampant with free love, with the desecration of those things that brought to these [Adam and Eve] in the beginning the knowledge of their existence, as to what may be termed—and at times became—the moral, or morality of a people.

Yet this same feeling, this same exaltation that comes from association of kindred bodies—that have their lives consecrated in a purposefulness, that makes for the ability of retaining those of the essence of creation in every virile body—can be made to become the fires that light truth, love, hope, patience, peace, harmony. For they are ever the key to those influences that fire the imaginations of those that are gifted in any form of depicting the high emotions of human experience, whether it be in the one or the other fields, and hence is judged by those that may not be able, or through desire submit themselves . . . to those elements, through the forces in the life about them. 364-6

Is marriage necessary and advisable?
    It is!
    When a man or woman has chosen (for it must be choice, and is only by choice that one remains out of relationships with the opposite sex in marriage)—if one has chosen to not be in such relationships, then be true to the choice [and live a celibate life]; or else it is to self a sin! For what one would pretend to be and isn't [such as a married person who violates his or her vows of fidelity] is indeed sin! 826-6

Our society favors monogamy but some other cultures approve of different forms of marital relationships? Is one superior to another?

Let the teachings be rather toward the spiritual intent [of those entering into such relationships, such as whether a man who takes one wife or more than one is a caring or an exploitive husband]. Whether it's monogamy, polygamy, or what not, let it be the answering of the spiritual within the individual!

But monogamy is the best, of course, as indicated from the Scripture itself—one—one! For the union of one should ever be one. 826-6

Would it be acceptable for a woman who desires to marry to be one of two or more wives to a man in a home rather than to remain alone and unmarried?

This is again a matter of principle; or the urge within such conditions must be conformative to the ideal [of love and kindness]. In the education of individuals as regarding sex relationships, as in every other educational activity, there must be a standard or a rule to go by or an ideal state that has its inception not in the emotions of a physical body but from the spiritual ideal [of unconditional love and commitment] which has been set, which was set and given to man in his relation to the Creative Forces. Then to ask or to seek or to advise or to give suggestions even, that it may be done outside of that, isn't being true to that as is presented. 826-6

Should men or women who don't have the opportunity to marry be free to have sexual relationships outside of marriage?

This again is a matter of principle within the individual. The sex organs, the sex demands of every individual, must be gratified in some manner as a portion of the biological urge within the individual. These begin in the present with curiosity. For it is as natural for there to be sexual relations between man and woman, when drawn together in their regular relations or activities, as it is for the flowers to bloom in the spring, or for the snows to come in the winter, when the atmospheric conditions are conducive or inductive to such conditions. 826-6

Can't sex relationships outside of marriage also be lovingly spiritual?

The relationships that come from that which is of the highest vibrations that are experienced in the material world are those that may be found in such relations, and [also] are the basis of what is termed the original sin; and hence may be easily misunderstood, misconstrued, misinterpreted in the experience of every individual; but these should be known—that the control of such, rather than being controlled by such, gives what makes for the awareness of spiritual intent and purpose. To overstep those conditions created by those environs in social relations and atmospheres that are brought about by such, however, is to take those leaves with self that may not be easily retained. Take not, give not, that that cannot be taken and given in the spirit of "His will, not mine, be done!" Each must judge such for themselves, in the light of their understanding. Each has the right to say I will, I will not. 911-5

How can one tell whether an intimate relationship is a spiritual experience or mainly physical?

Ask within [your]self, "What is the desire that is being gratified by the attributes of that relationship sought?" If it is the answer for those things that are an aggrandizement of self and self's own physical desires, then it is carnal or material. Is it for the creating of self as a channel for an expression of the spiritual influences that have been impelling and do impel the activities, then it is spiritual. 349-17

Is extramarital sex morally harmful?

This must ever be answered from one's own inner self. Those

attributes of procreation, of the pro-activity in individuals, are from the God force itself. The promptings of the inner man must ever be the guide; not from any source may there be given other than, "Study to show thyself approved unto the God that thou would worship." As you would have men do to you, do even so to them. In the light of your own understanding, keep your body pure, as you would have others keep their bodies pure. For your body is the temple of the living God. Do not desecrate same in your own consciousness. 826-2

Sexual urges vary from person to person, some are strong, others weak. What might be done when one partner has relatively strong desires compared to the other?

This must be met in the same way and manner as every other condition that brings for the body those harmful conditions, or conditions that tend to make it harder for the ills to be passed. Not that these desires are not to be gratified to the extent that makes for the developments in a normal manner, but to gratify any desire in the carnal [sexual] forces of the body—rather than in satisfying the spiritual life that comes of creation itself in such emotions—is to become such as one to make for the pricks that are to be kicked against time and time again.[9]

Self well understands that such gratification has been and is conducive and inducive to those periods of torments that arise at times; while with the applications in foods, in activities, with the outlets of self mentally and physically, these associations may be brought to mean much. Cultivate the spiritual, the mental, and [the] physical desire rather than those carnal desires that are gratified only for the moment. 911-7

9. In using a variation on the expression "kick against the pricks" (meaning to protest uselessly), Cayce apparently meant that to gratify sexual urges without satisfying their spiritual intent is unfulfilling.

When one partner loses desire for sex, but the other feels it is desirable or necessary, is there any solution?

Only in a united effort on the part of each to fill the need of each.[10] 2035-1

Is continence advisable, as in couples who don't want any more children?

For some, yes; in other cases it would be very bad on the part of each, while in others it would be bad on one or the other, see? [Repressing sexual desires might be emotionally distressing for some partners.] There should be, then, rather the educating as to the purposes [such as, to give greater attention to the children they already have, or to a creative endeavor that demands their full attention], and how—how that force, the vitality, that goes for the gratifying of emotions may be centralized in creating—in the lives of others about the body in all its various phases—spiritual blessings. [In short, how they might focus their creative energy on a worthy alternative to having (more) children, such as volunteering as a teacher's aide or working in a shelter for battered women and children.] 826-6

If a husband is impotent and doesn't respond to medication or other stimulants, would his wife be entitled to a sexual relationship with a trusted friend to help her carry on the normal business of home and work?

Such questions as these can only be answered in what is your ideal. Do not have an ideal and not attempt to reach same. There is no condemnation in those who do such for helpful forces, but if for personal, selfish gratification, it is sin....

---

10. Such a nonspecific response might seem puzzling, but it is Cayce's way of suggesting that the couple try to work it out as best they can, within the context of a caring relationship that respects the needs of both.

Keep self unspotted from the world. As to what the conduct should be, let it never be for only emotional satisfaction—but creative in its nature. 2329-1

Is celibacy recommended in some situations?

It is more advisable that each individual fulfill the purposes for which it entered the earthly experience. These include associations and relations with individuals in marital relationships, with most individuals. There are those for whom it is best that they keep a life of celibacy, owing to their circumstance and their activities. 2588-2

How can one best live a celibate life?

When [the kundalini] has arisen and is disseminated properly through the seven centers of the body, it has purified the body from all desire of sex relationships. For, this is an outlet through which one may attain to celibacy, through this activity. 2329-1

Is divorce a recommended option when incompatibilities can't be reconciled?

This depends upon first the education of the body [about the needs of a successful relationship]. Once united, once understood that the relationships are to be as one, less and less is there the necessity of such conditions [as divorce]. Man may learn a great deal from a study of the goose in this direction. Once it has mated, never is there a mating with any other—either the male or female, no matter how soon the destruction [death] of the mate may occur—unless forced by man's intervention.

This does not indicate that this is the end, and should only remain as such.... For this is the extreme. Just as indicated in all of the animals—the fowl or those that have become the closer related to man.... And from these man may learn many lessons; which was attempted in the beginning [in the Garden of Eden, or life on earth]. And yet, as we have indicated, in same he lost self in that he found that he could satisfy those emotions or gratify what might be built as emotions from experience to experience.

Thus there were gradually brought on the various polygamous relationships that have existed throughout the ages in many periods. And, as indicated in the lives of groups and nations, these become stumbling blocks that are ever kept within the background—but that have made for the destructive influence that arose within the activities of such groups and nations, in such relationships."826-6

Sexual relations are much freer today than a generation or two ago. Does anything concern you about this change?

The lack of education in the young before their teenage years! For few there be who have the proper understanding, as we have indicated, of what the biological urge produces in the body! Now whether such an education is to be undertaken in the home or in the school is the greater problem. 826-6

Sex education in the schools is controversial, for some sects oppose it entirely, and so the public schools avoid it.

To be sure, there are conditions existent in relationship to many of the denominational activities religiously that prohibit, bar, or prevent sufficient consideration of these problems in the public schools or even in the private schools. And little has there been of the proper education of the mother, the father of those who need such instruction. But these are the places to begin. And the warnings as would be presented are not as to the practices of this or the manner of that, or the association of this or that in the adult life. But there should be those precautions, understandings,

---

11. It is not known what groups Cayce referred to, perhaps the Mormons in nineteenth-century America who allowed polygamous marriages to build up their sect's numbers before polygamy was outlawed.

relationships as to how and in what manner there becomes the biological urge; which through the proper training may become a pathological condition in the body of the individual. For it is as from the beginning of puberty the essence of the Creative Forces or Energies within the body of the individual.…

And then, as these grow and become a portion of the body politic for public education, there should be greater stress laid upon the educations in these directions; and not wait until they have reached or arrived at that position where they begin to study physiology, anatomy, or hygiene. 826-6

So, you think it is up to the parents to begin sex education, and for the schools to finish the job?

In the formative years there should be training in these directions, as a portion of the material things. Even as the child studies its letters, let a portion of the instructions be in the care of the body, and more and more the stress upon the care in relation to the sex of the body and in the preservation of that as to its relationships to its Creator. For it is through such factors [as education] through such bodies of activity [schooling], that there may become a manifestation of the spiritual forces such as bring into being one's own flesh and blood. These are the approaches. These are the conditions [teach children early].

Do not begin halfway. Do not begin after [puberty when] there has been already begun the practice of the conditions [sexual activity] that make for destructive forces [unwanted pregnancies and/or sexually transmitted diseases], or for the issue of the body to become as a burning within the very elements of the body itself—and to find expression in the gratifying of the [carnal] emotions of the body! For, to be sure, relationships in sex are the exercising of the highest [most powerful] emotions in which a physical body may indulge. 826-6

Is teaching or preaching birth control helpful?

It is like shooting feathers at an eagle! It's a move in the right direction, but that's about as much as might be said. This should be rather the training of those [who] are in the positions of being the mothers and fathers of the nation, of the peoples!...

So with the education, so with that which does the prompting, let it be from not that which is lacking in an urge, but rather from what is to be done by the individual with the urge! See? and leave the results with the Giver of Life! For life is of, and is, the Creative Forces; it is that you worship God.

Those then that besmirch same [God] by overindulgence besmirch what is best within themselves [their own soul]. And that should be the key to birth control or sex relations, or every phase of the relationships between the sons and the daughters of men—that would become the sons and daughters of God. 826-6

What about nudism, or the partial nudism that passes for high fashion in some circles?

That should be a matter of principle within the individuals as there is the training as to what is the purpose of those parts covered. Nudism or clothing or what not, as we have often indicated, should be rather the matter of the environ—and not a matter of moral principle in any sense! 826-6

CHAPTER 4

❦

Holistic Healing

CAYCE HAS BEEN referred to as the "father of holistic medicine."
Put simply, holistic medicine is a revolutionary way of treating illness and disease that takes into account the patient's mental and
spiritual conditions as well as physical symptoms. At the heart of
Cayce's unique approach is a belief that the body is capable of
healing and sustaining itself when favorable conditions bring
body, mind, and spirit into balance. The healing arts merely assist
that natural process when needed.

What is the distinctive principle behind holistic healing?
   That the body-physical, the body-mental, and the body-
spiritual are one. 1443-1

*But if just the body is ailing, don't you treat it just as a physical ail-
ment?*
   All healing is of the spiritual, or within self. The influences [on
the human body come from within—a gift of the animating life
force—and] are the same as in all nature. [Thus, animals and
plants, no less than humans, benefit from healing energies from
within when properly nurtured.] 1019-1

So what do you prescribe for a sick person?

A portion of [whatever] elements we find lacking in the body [such as vitamins or minerals; otherwise]...there is the inability to resuscitate or to reproduce the resuscitation and the life forces. 1019-1

Don't you use medications to cure the patient?

No medicine, no appliance, cures. It only attunes the body for the activity of the living forces and living vibrations within the human system [allowing the body to heal naturally]. For every element that is necessary for the sustaining of health and of the co-ordination of same may be created within the body if each portion [bodily function, such as adequate circulation to remove wastes] is coordinating one with another. 1151-5

The public is bombarded with advertisements for prescription drugs that are said to bring relief from specific painful conditions such as arthritis. Are these not beneficial?

No....The causes [of the ailment] must be reached....Even the properties suggested [for such remedies] afford only temporary relief, unless the causes are corrected. So it is with...any properties supposed to supply energies to the body—it cannot be of great benefit unless the internal activity of the glandular force within the organ itself can be stimulated to produce the properties necessary to keep the normal balance.

Hence any exterior or superficial addition to the body [such as an anti-acid medication] is only temporary in its effect, unless we restore the activity of the source of supply so that it produces from the foods taken that to supply all portions of the body that are deficient. It is upon the source of supply [of energies] from within that the body depends for its resuscitation. Hence to rely upon exterior influences, or some compound to supply that which the body itself needs to create, is futile. Even if it offers temporary

benefit, it is not getting at the source of the trouble and other portions must eventually suffer. Hence it is futile to even *think* that
the condition will become normal under such applications—unless the cause is reached from within the body![12] 189-7

*What about such "wonder drugs" as penicillin? Haven't they healed
people of infectious diseases?*

No medicine, no mechanical appliance *does* the healing. It only
attunes the body to a perfect coordination [of the organs and their
functions] and the Divine gives the healing. For life is divine, and
each atom in a body that becomes cut off by disease... or an injury, then only needs awakening to its necessity of coordination,
cooperation with the other [parts]... to *fulfill* the purpose for
which the body, the soul, came into being.[13] 1546-1

*In other words, we need to respect the body's natural healing capabil-
ity?*

All that may be added to the body is only to enable each organ
to reproduce itself in a consistent way and manner, and it will get
rid of drosses [wastes or impurities] with its reproduction. For, as
in the spiritual life you grow in grace, in knowledge, in understanding of the law[s] of God, you also in the mental life grow in...
awareness of your associations with spiritual and material activi-

12. Under ideal conditions, the body can heal itself, but the reverse is also true:
deprived of essential needs it suffers. Simon Gabbay, in *Visionary Medicine*,
tells of patients in western New York suffering from severe myopathy, a muscle disorder that confined them to wheelchairs. When given high-potency vitamin D supplements, all patients improved within six weeks, and some
were able to walk free again. "Vitamin D deficiency is widespread...where
people don't get enough sunshine on a regular basis," writes Gabbay. "Poor
nutrition, fat-restricted diets, and intestinal malabsorption are other contributing factors."
13. Antibiotics, which are useful in combating serious infections, can also inter-
fere with the essential absorption of nutrients in the small intestines, thus re-
ducing the natural power of the immune system to ward off disease.

ties. So in the mental and spiritual, these throw off. For, have you not heard how that constantly there is the change, and that the body has in a seven-year cycle reproduced itself entirely? No need for anyone, then, to have *any* disturbance over that length of period, if by common sense there would be the care taken. But if your mind holds to it, and you've got a stumped toe, it will stay stumped! If you've got a bad condition in your gizzard, or liver, you'll keep it—if you think so. But the body—the physical, the mental, and [the] spiritual—will remove same, if you will *let* it and not hold to the disturbance! 257-249

I've known people who relied completely on natural healing and refused prescription drugs. Do you recommend that?

As we have indicated so often, when there are disturbances in the physical that are of a physical nature, these need to be tended to or treated, or application made, through physical means. There is as much of God in the physical as there is in the spiritual or mental, for it should be one! But it was necessary, when the Master [Jesus] demonstrated [during his various healings], to use what was needed in the bodies of individuals as curative forces as it was in the mental. To some He gave, "Thy sins be forgiven thee." To others He applied clay. To others they were dipped in water. To others, they must show themselves to the priest. . . .

These are one. Understand them as one, yet do not attempt, at all times, to heal with word [such as prayer] when mechanical [such as chiropractic adjustments] or other means are necessary to attune some disturbed portion with the mental and the spiritual forces of the body. Remember, the spirit is ever willing; the flesh is weak. 69-5

What place does the mind have in sickness and in healing?

Negative thought as well as sometimes negative reactions [such as anger or hostility] have allowed some of the disturbances [ailments] to become a constitutional condition [deleterious to the person's physique]. Hence these [negative factors] must be taken into consideration in the manner in which these have affected and do affect the functioning of the organs of the body itself.

It is very true that *mind* is the control, Mind is the builder, and mind may be made wholly a spiritual force or source. Yet remember, these [ailments] related to a physical being work through a physical organism, in every atom of which there are energies within themselves. Hence often there are the needs [in a malfunctioning organ]... that there be the application of the mechanical means [such as a chiropractic adjustment or a massage to stimulate circulation] as well as the influences that will work directly upon the functioning of the system as related to the physical body. 1471-1

Keep constructive influences and forces ever as a portion of the mental self [one's frame of mind]. Know that the mental forces [thoughts] are the builders, and that the attitude which is known by the body builds the environment [for the body]—and the environment makes the physical reactions. 979-9

You mean that our attitudes affect our health?

To be sure, attitudes often influence the physical conditions of the body. No one can hate his neighbor and not have stomach or liver trouble. No one can be jealous and allow the anger of same and not have upset digestion or heart disorder. 1074-1

For the body-physical-mental self, the Mind is the builder. The attitude individuals maintain, as an entity, toward conditions, individuals, and activities, creates that atmosphere for the supplying of energies from which has been taken the material for supplying the physical body.

Thusly, if one partakes of the fruit of the vine, or of cereal or of what not, and then holds the attitude of fire or *resentment* or animosity or hate—what can the spiritual and mental self do with such an attitude in those environs created by the attitude for such an assimilation or digestion in a body active in material forces! 1662-1

Keep the mental attitude in a constructive manner. Know within self that the physical elements may be built; that the mind is the builder; that the manner in which the spiritual influences and forces may act upon the system builds that which is held in the deeper mental force. Keep it, then, *constructive*! Do not think negatively. 1074-1

As to the attitudes, be not only good; but good *for* something, and this not only as related to self but in its relations to others. 3008-1

How do you go about spiritual healing?

A great deal has been and may be accomplished in the work, in the study of spiritual healing; and these should be kept as a part of the experience of each individual. Because there are periods when—with the associations of ideas, as well as ideals—it is necessary for the application of mechanical and medicinal properties in the experience of each. And, there are experiences when apparently there is the failure on the part of either [spiritual or medicinal] to bring material help to many, according to the *idea* [expectations for healing] of an individual. Such experiences [failures] have tended to create a laxness on the part of many [patients], and a questioning within self as to the need, or as to the use of it. 281-45

You mean that people may give up or become pessimistic if they don't see positive healing results in short order. So what is the alternative?

Be first consistent in your activities [treatment] and in your thoughts, and in your purposes, in your hopes, and in your desires day by day. And in the application of those truths, or those examples as were given by Him, as well as in your relationships to your fellows, be persistent, as well as consistent [to effect improvement]. 281-40

I assume you respect the power of prayer for healing, but what do you say to those who favor only the scientific methods of modern medicine?

Prayer is just as scientific as the knife, in its individual field. Mechano-therapy or mechanical treatments [chiropractic, osteopathy, or various forms of physical therapy] are as effective in their individual field, and are of the same source as prayer—if applied in the same way or manner, or with the same sincerity....

For those who desire to cause activities [with healing intent] through the influence of divine forces, let us consider: What were the methods used by Him [Jesus], upon whom each one calls? Just by speaking, just by prayer, just by fasting? No. Was there not anointing? Was there not washing? Was there not mechano-therapy? Were not even other conditions used in combination with them all? 1546-1

You're pointing out that Jesus, probably the world's most famous healer, applied whatever healing method was appropriate. I gather that you feel that while prayer is valuable and should be included when seeking a healing, it is not always sufficient. I say that because in one case you were asked if Christian Science alone would heal the ailing person. Tell us how you answered.

If it had been the most advisable, this alone would have been suggested. But let's have all the spiritual life, all the mental life, and [all] the physical life consistent [with one] another. For they each have their part in the whole. Just as Father, the Son, the Holy Spirit are the Godhead; so the Body, the Mind, the Soul (or the Spirit) are one in the physical body, but each performs that function in the consciousness of man, just as the Godhead does in man's indwelling in the earth. 1546-2

If mind is so central to healing, can the patient's will to live help in extreme illness?

By the treatment of the subconscious forces, which may be reached as the body rests, or as the sensuous consciousness is at suspension [while sleeping]. Suggestion then to the body reaches the will and the activity of the body; for, as in each and every individual, that from within must be awakened to bring the full resuscitation of physical reaction in the physical body; for whether there be applied mechanical, medicinal, or what not, the healing comes from within, and the awakening of that within brings the full coordination of the mental, the spiritual, the physical body— for even as a body is of the triune nature, each must foot, fulfill its own purpose; but at a *oneness* one with the other. Get that! 164-2

To get a better idea of your healing methodology, I've picked out one of your medical cases, a sixty-five-year-old woman suffering from Parkinson's disease for three years whom you examined in your unique way, while in a hypnotic trance. First of all, when you go into a trance, what is the source of the information you obtain?

[My] conscious mind becomes subjugated to the subconscious, superconscious, or soul-mind; and may and does communicate with like minds—and the subconscious or soul-force becomes universal. From any subconscious mind information may be obtained, either from this plane or from the impressions left by individuals that have gone on before. 3744-3

You mean that your subconscious connects with the subconscious of other persons, living or deceased, and gathers information stored in their subconscious or from impressions they've left behind, like footprints on the skein of time. What is contained in the subconscious mind?

The subconscious mind forgets nothing. The conscious mind receives the impression from without [through the five senses] and transfers all thought to the subconscious, where it remains even though the conscious be destroyed.[14] 294-1

In what form does this information come to you?

As we see a mirror reflecting direct[ly] that which is before it. It is not the object itself, but that reflected, as in this: The suggestion that reaches through to the subconscious or soul, in this state, gathers information from that reflected from what has been or is called real or material, whether of the material body or of the physical forces, and just as the mirror may be waved or bent to reflect in an obtuse manner, so that suggestion to the soul-forces may bend the reflection of what is given; yet within, the image itself is what is reflected and not that of some other.[15] 3744-3

Getting back to the woman with Parkinson's disease, what came through to you?

From the physical activity we [found] disturbing forces in this body of [1471]:

The blood supply indicates how that the toxic forces and the activities of the organs of assimilation and elimination have been and are clogged with the poisons of refuse forces in the system, until there are those specific reactions with the organs of the activity in the digestive forces.

Or in the gall duct area, the liver's activity and its coordination with the lower portion of the hepatic [liver] circulation, we have

14. Documents on file at the Association for Research and Enlightenment state that Cayce explained that his subconscious mind was in direct communication with all other subconscious minds and was able to interpret through his objective mind and impart his impressions to others, thus gathering all knowledge possessed by countless other subconscious minds.

15. Once again, not without difficulty, Cayce employs the mirror as a metaphor familiar to everyone to try to explain what is hard for most of us to fathom, namely the mystical delivery of images that reach him from other sources during a trance.

such as to produce those contractions in the muscular forces throughout this disturbed circulation; until we have both an arthritic and a neurotic reaction or activity.

Hence there are periods or times, and especially under some stresses or strains, when the very movements or activities of the body, or the pressures from the activity of the atmospheric reactions, produce contraction and pains and disturbance and distress—or stress—upon the whole of the nervous systems of the body; until there are *acute* pains. These are also indicated in the effect of the natural reactions these have upon other portions of the system, as in the sensory organism of the body. All of these become a part of the disturbing forces. 1471-1

It is amazing that you were able to obtain such a vivid picture of these malfunctioning organs of this woman's body without using any instruments or even touching her. What else did you find?

From the congestion and the activities of the poisons as indicated in the blood supply, these make for pressures upon the nerve system and systems of the body; especially in those areas or ganglia, or the locomotory axis and centers we find conditions where the extremities become involved in the disturbances themselves. And these produce, to be sure, the greater disturbance in locomotion or activity or physical exercise or exertion. These all become a part of the whole or general condition, but are effects rather than causes; the causes arising from the conditions as we have indicated.

In the activities of organs themselves, as has been indicated, more specifically these arise from the functioning of the hepatic circulation as related to the deeper and also to the superficial circulation—with the effect produced upon the sensory system by their pressures or activity upon the superficial or vegetative nerve systems of the body. Hence the organs of the sensory forces—

eyes, ears, taste, feeling, effects upon the whole of the system or as related to the senses—become involved in the condition. 1471-1

What did you recommend for this patient?

Begin first with the Cabinet Sweats [a steambath], followed with the Fume Baths of specific nature [steam bath with a medicinal additive such as camphor]. The Fume Baths would be taken twice a week, but one time use the fumes from Tincture of Iodine and the next time Spirits of Camphor—a tablespoonful to half a pint of water, and let this be allowed to steam as from a vapor cup *following* the Cabinet Bath when the body has been relaxed by the heat from same, see? And the Fume Bath would require only a few minutes—fifteen to twenty minutes.

But following the Cabinet and the Fume Bath—after both have been taken, at the same time, you see—or both of these taken twice a week—we would have a thorough massage and rubdown, for these will greatly aid in the superficial circulation, by the manner of such manipulations or massages.

Each day we would use also the activities of the Radio-Active Appliance[16] that will enable the body to rest—if the attachments are kept properly in their order of circulation about the body, in the applications of the anodes for the activities of same. Use the appliance for thirty minutes to an hour each day, for periods of three to four weeks, leave off a week or ten days, and then take again for periods of three to four weeks. Keep the anodes clean. Make the circle about the body with the attachments; that is, right wrist, left ankle; left wrist, right ankle; left ankle, right wrist; right

16. A unique battery-like device often recommended by Cayce to modulate the body's electrical energy field, promoting relaxation, improving circulation, and balancing the body. Using Cayce's detailed instructions of how to make the Radio-Active Appliance, it was manufactured privately and distributed to Cayce subscribers.

ankle, left wrist—then begin with the right wrist and left ankle again, and so on, around the body.

We find that the diet would be much in keeping with what has been indicated. The vegetables, the fruits, and the nuts, prefer-ably—instead of too great quantities of meats; though fish, fowl, and lamb may be included in such proportions as will not only satisfy but will build the necessary influences for the activities of the other properties upon the bodily forces themselves.

Do these; then after sixty to ninety days we would give further instructions for this particular disturbance. Do that. 1471-1

With all due respect for your remarkable record helping people whose regular doctors failed them, you are not a medical doctor, nor were you trained in anatomy or physiology. Why should anyone accept your di-agnosis or prescription?

Consider the fact that there was first the study, the meditation and prayer upon His word, which brought that desire, that hope, that purpose to give self as a channel through which help might come to those who would in Him seek for the betterment of their physical forces and conditions. Then consider the vision [that Cayce had as a boy], the spoken word [from a spirit he envisioned]: "Ask! What seekest thou? What desirest thou to do?" 294-202

Yes, I recall that in your authorized biography, There Is a River *by Thomas Sugrue, he wrote about your having had a vision of an angelic figure who asked what you most wanted. And what did you tell her was your wish?*

The desire was that there might be the ability to help others who were ill, especially children. 294-202

What was her reaction?

Then [she said]: "Thy prayer has been heard." 294-202

Do you think that is why you have this phenomenal diagnostic and healing gift?

The results through the years speak for themselves.[17] 294-202

You say your subconscious tunes into the subconscious of the patient who is seeking your help. How does that help?

Who knows better than the individuals themselves what has hindered them from being physically, mentally, [and] spiritually in accord with the divine that *is* life manifested in the body? 294-202

You mean that we know subconsciously at some deep level of our being what is wrong or why we are ill?

Are we not all children of God? Are we not co-creators with Him? Have we not been with Him from the beginning? Is there any knowledge, wisdom, or understanding withheld if we have attuned ourself to [the] Creative Forces which made the worlds and all the forces manifested in same? Do you think that the arm of God is ever short with you because you have erred? "Though ye be afar, though ye be in the uttermost parts, if ye call I will hear! and answer speedily." Do you think that speaks of another, or to you? 294-202

But how can we access that information for ourselves without getting a psychic reading from someone like you?

Open your mind, your heart, your purpose to your God and His purpose with you.

As to why this or that information may be indicated often to individuals through this channel, this may be determined by those who analyze same from a practical, material experience—as a psy-

17. Cayce gave more than 9,500 health readings during the forty years after realizing his gift for healing.

chiatrist, a psychoanalyst. An individual who understands the pathology of a physical body is taken where he is, and is supplied that information which if applied in that condition existent will be helpful in his relationship to that he worships!

God seeks all to be one with Him. And as all things were made by Him, that which is the creative influence in every herb, mineral, vegetable, or individual activity *is* that same force we call God—and *seeks* expression! Even as when God said, "Let there be light," and there was light. For, this is law; this is love.

Hence those who seek in sincerity, in hope, in purpose, to know, to receive; only to the measure that they manifest their hope, their belief, their desire in a God-purpose through a promise made to a man! Thus you have the source. Thus you have the manner. The seeker answers. For, know you, all: You give an account to God for every deed, for every idle word, for every purposeful hope you have made manifest. 294-202

Your concept of healing is quite different from what most of us assume when we take a pill in hopes it will make us well. How is it that our physical bodies can heal wounds and even some diseases if properly cared for?

Know that all strength, all healing of every nature is the changing of the vibrations from within, the attuning of the divine within the living tissue of a body to Creative Energies. This alone is healing. Whether it is accomplished by the use of drugs, the knife, or what not, it is the attuning of the atomic structure of the living cellular force to its spiritual heritage [so that the body functions as intended by the Creator]. 1967-1

The physical body is an atomic structure subject to the laws of its environment, its heredity, its *soul* development. The activity of healing, then, is to create or make a balance in the necessary units of the influence or force [body energy] that is set in motion as the body in material form, through the motivative force of spiritual activity [life force], sets in motion. It is seen that each atom, each corpuscle, has within it the whole form of the universe—within its *own* structure. [Healing is achieved by balancing all units of the body so that they function as intended.]

As for the *physical* body, this is made up of the elements of the various natures that keep it in its motion necessary for sustaining its equilibrium; as begun from its (the individual body's) first cause. If in the atomic forces there becomes an overbalancing, an injury, a happening, an accident, there are certain atomic forces destroyed or others increased; that to the physical body become either such as to add to or take from the "elan vitale" [vitality] that makes for the motivative forces through that particular or individual activity.

Then, in meeting these it becomes necessary for the creating of that influence within each individual body to bring a balance necessary for its continued activity about each of the atomic centers its own rotary [motion] or creative force, its own elements for the ability of resuscitating, revivifying, such influence or force in the body. 281-24

Can ordinary people learn to tune into one another to help whoever is sick?

When a body, separate from that one ill, then, has so attuned or raised its own vibrations sufficiently [through meditation, perhaps], it may—by the motion of the spoken word [such as prayer]—awaken the activity of the emotions to such an extent as to revivify, resuscitate, or to change the rotary force [vibrations] or influence or the atomic forces in the activity of the structural portion, or the vital forces of a body, in such a way and manner as to set it again in motion.

Thus does spiritual or psychic influence of body upon body [one person for another] bring healing to any individual; where another body may raise that necessary influence in the hormone

of the circulatory forces as to take from that within itself to revivify or resuscitate diseased, disordered, or distressed conditions
within a body. For, as has been often said, any manner in which
healing comes—whether by the laying on of hands, prayer, by a
look, by the application of any mechanical influence or any of
those forces in materia medica [medicinal drugs]—must be of
such a nature as to produce what is necessary within those forces
about the atomic centers of a given body for it to bring resuscitating or healing.

The law, then, is compliance with the universal spiritual influence that awakens any atomic center to the necessity of its con-
current activity in relationships to other pathological forces or
influences within a given body [so that the body's natural vibratory energies overcome the pathology of disease]. Whether this is
by spiritual forces, by any of the mechanical forces, it is of necessity one and the same. Many are the divisions or characters [types
and nature] of those ills that befall or become a portion of each individual body. Some are set in motion so that certain portions of
the glandular system or of the organs of the body perform more
than their share. Hence some [people] are thin, some are fat,
some are tall, some are short. Can anyone by taking thought make
one hair white or black, or add one cubit to his stature? [Evidently
not.]

Who gives healing, then? It is in any manner the result only of
compliance to the First Cause [God], and the activity of same
within the individual's relative relation to its own evolution. 281-24

*How can an individual raise his own vibrations, or whatever may be
necessary, to effect a healing?*

By raising that attunement of self to the spirit within, that is of
the soul-body. Often in those conditions where necessary we have
seen produced within a body unusual or abnormal strength, either for physical or mental activity. From whence arose such?

Who has given the power? Within what live you? What is Life? Is it the *attuning* of self, then, to same. How?

As the body-physical is purified, as the mental body is made wholly at-one with purification or purity, with the life and light within itself, healing comes, strength comes, power comes.

So may an individual effect a healing, through meditation, through attuning not just a side of the mind nor a portion of the body but the whole, to that at-oneness with the spiritual forces within, the gift of the life force within each body? For when matter comes into being, what has taken place? The Spirit you worship as God has *moved* in space and in time to make what gives its expression; perhaps as wheat, as corn, as flesh, as whatever may be the movement in what you call time and space.

Then *making* self in an at-onement with that Creative Force brings what? That necessary for the activity which has been set in motion and has become manifested to be in accord *with* that First Cause.

Hence we find it becomes necessary that you speak, you act, that way. For whoever comes to offer to self, or to make an offering to the throne of mercy or grace, and speaks unkindly of his brother, is only partially awake or aware. For what has brought distraughtness, distress, disease in the earth, or in manifestation, is transgression of the law. 281-24

In reviewing a number of the medical cases in your files, I noticed one for a sixty-eight-year-old man that seems to illustrate your emphasis on taking a holistic approach. Would you describe the conditions you found for case 1245?

There have been and are disturbances in the physical forces of this body where there has been and is an unbalancing of the elements in the system as pertain to the activity or the functioning of organs in relation to the eliminating and assimilating forces of the body. Thus through the drosses that have been as accumulations, the taxation to the portions of the system—as of the hepatic circulation as related to the lymphatic and the superficial circulation—has caused and does cause those disorders in portions of the extremities.

As we find then, if there would be the addition into the system of those influences or properties that make for a coordinant activity between the pathological, the psychological, the mental, and the influences to make for an equal balance, these will be helpful—for we find these are in their inception and in their sources of the *One Source*! For life itself in its manifestations in or through matter is of that creative energy or influence which is manifested in, or called by man as the God force in man. 1245-1

I suppose it's not uncommon for ailments to stem from a lack of coordination of the mental and physical forces. What do you do to relieve such conditions?

Hence those from animal, mineral, vegetable kingdoms or forces as may be combined in compounds that may be activative with the influences of the system, then, are in their inception, in their basic force, from the same source of life itself. For they, as an influence, work with or work against—as has been seen by the unbalancing of the forces in this system itself.

Hence as we have in this body a blood supply that is abnormal in its pressure, we have an activity through the hepatic circulation as an unbalanced condition by the elements or salts and influences of the forces in the body, then to bring about a better coordination in these:

We would find that the adding then of these in the system in the proportion and in the manner as we would indicate here would bring about a feeling of not only relief but give the physical and mental forces of the body the greater opportunity for their expression among the physical forces and physical beings that are—as self—a manifestation of that influence, that force of Good that represents, or is a manifestation of the creative energies or forces in the air and in matter itself. 1245-1

There are instances where you believed that no medicines are required—how did you determine that?

This will depend upon the general eliminations or the general activity. The less medications, *as* medicines, the better it will be for the body; provided these are not necessary to add stimulation to some depleted or defunct activity of an organ or for the strengthening of the body in some way or manner. But these are rather as tonics and stimulants than as medications, we find. For nature should be the healer. 1245-1

What do you recommend for self-healing and remaining well and strong?

Much may be given respecting the choice, the desire of the body in its willingness to be a channel through which greater spiritual enlightenment may come. It is a choice that is well for the entity, for the body; for the peace and harmony that such may bring into the experience of the entity.

Then, we would approach each phase from its own activity and relationship. As is understood by the entity, each must coordinate—one with another. Then, in the practice and in the application of the fruit of the spirit we find that the desire and the purpose may be made a practical experience for the entity in its activities among its fellow men.

First, the physical body is the temple, the encasement of the mind and soul of the entity. It has its virtues, its faults, its weaknesses, its strengths. Yet, as is understood, he that is wholly—mentally, spiritually—in accord with the oneness of the Christ-consciousness may expect and may live and may know within self the *proper* course for the activities to bring the best welfare for the body.

But that these may be fortified, that the mental self may be assured...these may be strengthened that the higher spiritual and mental self may have then the better, the greater channel through which to magnify the spirit of truth that may indeed set not only self but others free in this material experience....

Each of these phases must be met in its own scope and sphere of activity. Then, by following nature's courses as there is given the mental body to feed upon, this or that spiritual or natural law, so does it apply same in its relationships to self as to others; also the material or natural laws respecting the physical body.

Keep same then clear, clean from those defects or deficiencies that would hinder in the natural processes of resuscitating and reviving its own self; supplying sufficient of energies; keeping a balance between the natural salts of the body itself so that the chemical reaction within same is purified.

Thus, not such a diet as to be contrary to natural laws, but that which is in keeping with the manner in which the body exerts self—so that there may be brought the better resuscitating influences and forces. 1662-1

How about physical exercise for keeping fit?

Have sufficient activity between the meals so that the bodily energies have sufficient exercise to keep a normal balance, thus using up the energies as created by that which has been taken into the system for activity.

Do these, combining same with the seeking as would be a part of the regular activity to keep and maintain and build a better resistance in the influence of the physical forces of the body—in these activities through this material experience. 1662-1

As alternative medicine has become more acceptable to the public in recent years, a number of allopathic physicians have accepted some holistic measures such as meditation. Many other doctors reject anything outside the mainstream pharmaceutical remedies. Do you think some-day medical schools will teach a system of universal medicine, where all methods of healing are combined?

The ground for same may be laid, or the activities for same begun. But so many prejudices exist in so many fields, there is so much selfishness—not only in one school but in many schools—that this becomes almost a hopeless task.

That such an institution is the ideal manner goes without question; for there is Good in all methods—and they have their place. But from whence comes the healing? Whether there is administered a drug, a correcting or an adjustment of a subluxation, or the alleviating of a strain upon the muscles, or the revivifying through electrical forces; they are one, and the healing comes from within. Not by the method does the healing come, though the consciousness of the individual is such that this or that method is the one that is more effective in the individual case in arousing the forces from within. But methods are not ideals. The ideal must be kept in the proper source; and then this ideal may be gradually instilled into the laity in such measures and manners that there may be gradually built what would stand as an ideal manner. 969-1

In 1927 you predicted that medical science would make great advances in diagnostics, do you remember that?

The day may yet arrive when one may take a drop of blood and diagnose the condition of any physical body. 283-2

I often think of that when I go to the Virginia Beach Diagnostic Center and they take a blood sample to check on the state of many of my vital organs. Certainly great strides are being made in analyzing the blood to monitor our health.

What's the most important thing to keep in mind when it comes to holistic healing?

Remember, healing, all healing comes from within. Yet there

is the healing of the physical, there is the healing of the mental, [and] there is the correct direction from the spirit. Coordinate these and you'll be whole! But to attempt to do a physical healing through the mental conditions [without regard for spiritual ideals] is the misdirection of the spirit that prompts same—the same that brings about accidents, the same that brings about the eventual separation [death]. For it is *law* [that we are spiritual beings]. But when the law is coordinated, in spirit, in mind, in body, the entity is capable of fulfilling the purpose for which it enters a material or physical experience. 2528-2

CHAPTER 5

The Cayce Diet

LONG BEFORE DIETING for weight control or even for the nutritional boost to good health preoccupied many Americans, Cayce prescribed a diet that was heavy in fruits and vegetables and light on meats that he said offered our bodies what they most needed to enjoy vitality and avoid illness.

When people say they follow your diet recommendations, they seem to have broad objectives in mind such as overall good health rather than weight loss. What are the main features of the Cayce diet?

Whole grain cereals, plenty of citrus fruits, plenty of fresh fruits and fresh vegetables. Plenty of seafoods in their proper season and their proper relation one to another. These we find in the main are the better conditions [for good health]. 257-252

You didn't mention meat—is meat acceptable?

Of course, [but] as the body has learned, be mindful of not eating heavy meats when under stress or strain. 696-2

What would an average person on your diet eat each day?

Those [foods] that are naturally easily assimilated and that make for increase in the lymph and the blood flow—as we would find in this character of an outline, though this may be changed or altered—it is only given as a basis:

Of mornings, have citrus fruits often, with hot cakes, eggs, bacon or the like, or alter to cereals—both dry and cooked; but do not take these the same day that the citrus fruits are taken.

At least three mornings each week we would have the rolled or crushed or cracked whole wheat [hot cereal], that is not cooked too long so as to destroy the whole vitamin force in same, but this will add to the body the proper proportions of iron, silicon, and the vitamins necessary to build up the blood supply that makes for resistance in the system. At other periods have citrus fruits, citrus fruit juices, the yolk of eggs (preferably soft-boiled or coddled— not the white portions of same), browned bread with butter, Ovaltine or milk; or coffee, provided there is no milk or cream put in the coffee. Occasionally stewed fruits, as baked apples with cream, stewed figs, stewed raisins, stewed prunes, or stewed apricots. But do not eat citrus fruits at the same meal with cereals or gruels or any of the breakfast foods. 840-1

What about lunch?

If practical, either soups, green vegetables or the like. 1467-11

Do you mean cooked vegetables?

Preferably raw fresh vegetables; none cooked at this meal. These would consist of tomatoes, lettuce, celery, spinach, carrots, beet tops, mustard, onions or the like (not cucumbers) that make for purifying of the humor [fluid] in the lymph blood as this is absorbed by the lacteal ducts as it is digested. 840-1

There should be at least one meal a day of only raw fresh vegetables, whether in the middle of the day or whether in the evening; preferably in the noonday time would this meal be taken. 1276-1

This is for creating a balance [in nutritional values benefiting the system]. At first it will tend to appear to create gas, but keep on using. 404-7

Vegetables dominate your diet, don't they?

Plenty of the fresh raw vegetables—such as carrots, celery, lettuce, radish—if these all agree with the body. Not in large quantities, but some of either or all of these each day. 2831-3

Have at least two leafy vegetables to one grown under the ground or of the pod nature. 3229-1

Often use the raw vegetables which are prepared with [a sprinkling of uncooked] gelatin. Use these at least three times each week. Those which grow more above the ground than those which grow below the ground. Do include, when these are prepared, carrots with that portion especially close to the top. It may appear the harder and the less desirable but it carries the vital energies, stimulating the optic reactions between kidneys and the optics. 3051-6

Keep to those things that heal within and without. A great deal of celery, lettuce, tomatoes, and especially use the garden blueberry. (This is a property which someone, some day, will use in its proper place!)[18] These should be stewed, but with their own juices, little sugar but in their own juices. Also use plenty of watercress, beets, and especially beet tops. These, of course, are to be used in sufficient quantity to satisfy the appetite but not to make any of them become something disliked. So prepare them in many different forms. 3118-1

---

18. Nutritional values abound in blueberries: a cupful offers a fat-free, cholesterol-free, sodium-free tasty treat providing vitamin C (15 percent of your daily requirement), plus a high source of dietary fiber with 5 grams, or 20 percent, of your daily value, and only 80 calories.

You'd be encouraged by the popularity of salad bars in restaurants and food markets today, which indicates that many people are not satisfied with a fast-food burger for lunch.

Vegetables that are green and raw, and fruits and nuts, are much preferable to meats or any greases of any kind; for these tend to make—for in the activity of the blood supply—a humor that irritates the nerve forces of the system. 162-2

We would also in the middle period have dried milk, preferable to raw milk, in which there would be carried such as egg. 642-1

That leaves dinner as the main meal. What can you have?

Evenings, plenty of cooked vegetables, more of the leafy than the pod or tuberous—these are preferable. Fish, fowl, and lamb are preferable for meats, but occasionally a good, thick steak—but cook it *well*. Very seldom have hog meat, though liver, the pigs' feet, the ear, any of those portions that are the digestive foods, that are palatable for the body, are very good—if prepared properly. 1467-11

Many people have adopted a diet that recommends lots of meat for protein. What do you think of that?

Meats—only occasionally; preferably, when taken—if taken—fowl, fish or lamb. 1468-5

Then we would have the beef juice occasionally; not broth, but the pure beef juice; and fish, or those that will supply more of iodine in an absorbent manner. 2831-3

What is the best meat substitute?

Soy beans. 257-252

Is there anything other than soy beans that take the place of meat?

Any of those combinations that carry a great amount of the

vital forces are good [such as fish and fowl], but there is no substitute for meats for a body that has become accustomed to it.
257-252

Are there other foods or combinations we should avoid?
No fried foods at all. 1276-1 Do not combine potatoes with rice
or spaghetti or white bread, or if either or any one of these is taken
do not eat meat at that meal! Do not combine great quantities of
starches with large quantities of sweets, or fats; but [small] portions of these are well to be taken. 1468-5 In keeping these, then,
we will find that we will also aid in keeping a balance through
eliminations. 1276-1
Make at times a meal upon fruits only. At others of vegetables
only. At others practically of meats only, with only sufficient of the
others to make a balanced meal. 877-13
Very light foods while traveling. No heavy foods at all. 257-247

*Many people carry water bottles with them all day long. Are they over-
doing it?*
Drink plenty of water at all times. 1206-11.

Does soda water count?
Refrain from carbonated waters or any drinks made with
same. 2585-1

And what do you think about alcoholic beverages?
Can you stop when you want to? Some can, some can't! Be always in *control* of what may be of the most beneficent effects to
the human body. 440-15

*Do you agree with those who recommend drinking in moderation as
beneficial to the health of those who can control it?*

A glass of wine a day is helpful; that is, not too big a glass. 365-4 Wine taken in excess—of course—is harmful; wine taken with bread alone is body, blood and nerve and brain building. 821-1

Would a drink before bedtime help as a relaxant?
Not when retiring; but about two ounces of red wine in the late afternoon—with black or brown bread—would be very, *very* well. 340-31 A little red wine *as a food*, but not as a stimulant, is alright occasionally; that is, taken in the late afternoon or evening with black or brown bread. 454-8 or with Ry-Krisp or the like... About a jigger or half a jigger at a time. 528-6 Hard drinks are not so well. These disturb the equilibrium through the activity of the liver itself. 877-8

What kind of wine?
That which is well fermented, or grape juices or the like; these are the better, not too much of the sour nor too sweet a wine. Tokay, Port, Sauterne. 821-1 The lighter wines or champagne should be *sipped*, as to make for a settling of the stomach and to strengthen the body. 325-60

Speaking of stimulants, what about coffee and tea?
Coffee is better than tea, though the body may prefer the tea. Coffee without milk and without sugar is preferable; but coffee without cream or milk *is* a food value. There is very little food value in tea, though it is a stimulant. Coffee is preferable. 462-6

How important are vitamins?
Have a regular well-balanced diet, with plenty especially of vitamins A, B-1, and G; these from reinforced grains or flour, or any of the yellow foods, or especially fowl—the bony pieces [wings and legs], fish, and liver, pigs' feet or pigs' ears, but not the rest of the hog. 1532-4

What do you mean by a "well-balanced" diet?

That is, let the food values be 80 percent alkaline to 20 percent acid-producing for the system. Do not give white breads or too much starches; as corn or beans, nor too much of raw milk—though dry milk or Dryco or malted milk may be used, those brands that are desiccated or that are particularly body, blood and nerve building as to the activity of vitamins added to same. These we find are preferable for the body. Fruits, and nuts in moderation.

But keep for a normal balance of the alkaline[19] reaction. Not that no meats should ever be taken; for fowl, fish, mutton or lamb are well. But other types are not so well. Wild game in its regular season is well. Keep a well-balanced vegetable diet, making for the correct balance; that is, not that it becomes rote, but watch self. If too great a combination of such as peas, lentils, beans, carrots, becomes a hardship or produces—as from the natural coloring, the natural manner in which these are prepared—irritation through the creating of an effluvium [a gaseous waste product] in the blood stream, it is not that the food *value* itself is wrong; possibly it's the preparation! These should be noted and watched by the body. For all of these especially as indicated are well for the body, though they do make disturbances in their preparation. There is a vast difference in the effect they create upon the body itself when prepared differently! For carrots, both raw and cooked, are helpful—and helpful elements of a special nature that are especially good for the body. But there should be almost as many eaten raw as there are cooked! And when cooked, not with a lot of others, but in their own juices! For these are the better.[20] 1000-12

19. Cayce recommended a diet of 80 percent alkaline-forming foods, such as fruits and vegetables that leave alkaline-forming mineral elements in the body. Meats, grains, most fats, and dairy products produce an acid residue. A chart of the acid- and alkaline-producing foods is available from the Association for Research and Enlightenment, 215 67th St., Virginia Beach, VA 23451.

20. For suggestions on how to prepare foods and retain their nutritional value, see *How to Cook It Right* by Adelle Davis.

Some studies show that the quantity of food one eats affects our health, notably our weight. Some Europeans, especially the French, seem to benefit by eating smaller portions. Do you have any thoughts on this?

Be mindful that there are not excesses at any time, either in extraordinary dieting (that is, refraining from this or that or the other, from conditions to produce reactions) or in overeating in any direction; but keep rather a nominal, normal balance in the diet—not excesses. Not excesses of those that produce then a form of alcohol in the system, as excesses of sugars with starches, or excesses of meats. Beware of too much seafood, but it is well to occasionally have those effects of glandular cleansing as from iodine reaction in the system.

Those things that will work then with the digestive forces, those that work with the nerve energies, those that make for keeping a balance in these physical ways, as we find would be the more preferable and helpful to the body—with the precautions mentally and physically in its exercise. 694-3

What do you suggest for those who are overweight and would like to lose a few pounds?

Four times each day, about half an hour before each meal and at bedtime, drink two ounces of grape juice (Welch's, preferably) in one ounce of plain water (not carbonated water). This will make for better assimilation, better elimination, and better conditions throughout the system. 2067-3

What does grape juice do?

[It] creates a better metabolism and katabolism [breaking down in living organisms of complex substances into simpler ones with the release of energy]. We will make for the better eliminations. We will find better conditions through the whole of the reactions in the physical forces of the body. 2067-3

Any other suggestions for weight loss?

If the body will use the RyKrisp or such mostly as the bread, and take before the evening meal at least half to an hour before... this would materially reduce the desire for foods that tend to produce flesh. Keep away, of course, from the high starches. 420-71

Your food suggestions are generally designed to maintain good health, but are there other considerations to keep in mind when planning meals?

In the physical body, be mindful to keep proper eliminations. As in the experience of most individuals during the elderly portion of the life, the lagging of this or that phase of the eliminating activity finds its reaction in the body forces. 257-252

The system always, as life itself, attempts to use the best it has to do the best it can with what it has to do with. Hence create a balance in the vitamins and in the amount of the necessary foods for creating a sufficient quantity of heat [calories], but also sufficient quantity of eliminating forces [such as fiber], see? 642-1

What foods do you suggest for improving regularity in elimination?

Prunes or eggplant, or pie plant stewed [rhubarb pie] to be sure will assist. These should be taken about once a week, and... will work well together if they are taken about this often. 569-25

Raw foods often [are] the foods which tend towards better eliminations; figs; pie plant prepare this in the different forms; senna leaves, senna pods, all of these may be parts of the diet at various periods. We will find as the ideals are set, what are your ideal eliminations? Once a day, twice a day or the activities of the liver, activities of kidneys, the activities of digestion and assimilation and the drosses which should be eliminated. Do not lay such a great stress on these that you find mind applying self as, "I can't do this and I can't do that or I can't do the other" but being rational and normal in keeping with conditions which develop. 3051-6

The diet should be wholesome but not too rich foods at any time; that is, not the fats of meats. 3195-1

To keep the kidneys in better activity, about every Wednesday take watermelon seed tea. Crush the seed, about a half an ounce of same, put in a pint of water. Let this brew as tea. This may be strained and set aside, but do not keep longer, even in the ice box, than two or three days; for this becomes then retroactive, of course, by the action of air and of properties that would be in the same location throwing off their emanations. It is better that it be put in a bottle and corked, even in the ice box, when kept at all; but warmed to be taken. It would only be taken once a week for several weeks, not to overflow but to make more of an activity in these eliminations.

Do these as we find for the better conditions of this body. 569-25

Are desserts a no-no, or are some sweets acceptable?

Never very much of any confection or pastry or cake. 3195-1 When sweets are taken, we find that honey or maple sugar, or candies made with beet sugar, are preferable to cane sugar.

Eat honey in the honeycomb as a sweet, and be sure there is the comb in most of that eaten; for this, with other conditions, will assist in better purifying through the alimentary canal, for it acts as an aid to better conditions, and will not disturb the pancreas and the kidneys; but works better with corn bread or whole wheat bread, that are better as breads than the white bread. 569-25

Your diet suggestions, unless one likes lots of red meat and French fries, seem less restrictive than some other diets that are quite strict.

Do not become so diet-conscious as for the diet to become master, rather than the self being master of the diet. 2454-1

You allow for flexibility, even an occasional indulgence, I take it?

In the matter of diet itself, we would have this as an outline, though—to be sure—this may be altered from time to time to suit the tastes of the body. 840-1

What do you say to people who eat sensibly and don't need to lose weight?

Eat what the appetite calls for—and whatever it calls for; but don't overload, of course. 696-2

You cautioned about eating heavy foods while under stress. Is our mental outlook a factor to consider when eating?

Keep in that of constructive thought; because, to be sure, the thoughts of the body act upon the emotions as well as the assimilating forces. Poisons are accumulated or produced by anger or by resentment or animosity. Keep sweet! 23-3

The demonstration to be made is better cooperation in body, mind, and spirit or soul of the entity. Thus, as has been given: Definite decisions in self as to attitudes towards all activities of body, mind and purpose, or the choosing of the ideals. In choosing same for the body, don't trust to the memory, don't trust to the thinking that "this I believe," for you change it often, but write it down: Body. Mind. Soul. Begin with the soul, what is your ideal? The answer must be within self and of Jesus, the Christ. This, to be sure, is first, last and always.

Then, what is the ideal mentally? This should be: How much meditation, how much application, how much appreciation. These, as we find, may be subdivided or, as changes come each day, rub out and change. What is the mind and the spirit as referred to body ideal? See the body perfect in vision, in thought, in purpose. This is now the purpose of physical, not purpose of the mental. 3051-6

So, it is not only what is on our dinner plate that affects our health but what is on our minds while eating, especially if we are in an unhappy emotional state. Some things are bound to set us off, so what do we do?

Beware of those influences, then, when anger rules the tongue. 1347-1

Many people today exercise in one way or another in order to stay physically fit. Some go to gyms and work out on machines, others jog or walk near their homes. What do you recommend?

There's no exercise better than walking or rowing or golfing! 257-200

How far should we walk every day?

Whether it's a mile or a step, do that which makes for a better "feel" for the body; getting into the open! Know something of nature. How many kinds of trees do you know? . . . How many kinds of birds do you know? . . . Do you know the call of any? Interest self in all nature! 257-204

Many of us walk a lot in our work. Does that count, too?

There should be more exercise, but this is very good. Walk a good deal in the sunshine. 257-238

Regular periods of walking and regular periods for the setting up exercises would be very well for keeping the body trim or preventing abdominal growth or on any portion of the body. Stretch the body as a cat would stretch. This is the best exercise to keep body in proportion. 5271-1

What other exercises are helpful?

The exercises should be of a specific nature. Mornings, exercise the upper portion of the body—head, neck, shoulders—rotation of head, back, forward, side, circle—both ways—at least eight to ten times, and take time to do it! Also in the evenings, when ready for retiring, the circular motion of the body below the diaphragm, so that the muscles of the abdomen and of the locomotories in the lower portion of the body may be relaxed sufficient that the body will rest easier. 5459-4

So, as we find, if the exercises that are not of too strenuous a nature taken consistently morning and evening, for two, three, four minutes, we would find quite a change in the bodily reactions. Of morning they would be in this manner:

Upon arising, standing erect, stretch slowly, easily, the hands as high above the head as possible. Bending forward without bending the knees, three, four, five, six, eight to ten times, slowly, not exercising too heavily. When raising the hands, rise gently on the toes, you see. Inhale as the body stretches itself upward. Exhale through the mouth as the body bends forward.

In the evening alter the exercise to this, just before retiring! Begin with the head and neck exercises, preferably with the hands upon the hips. Turning the head one, two, three times to the left, gently. One, two, three to the right. One, two, three to the front. One, two, three to the back. Then circulate the bodily forces from the waist almost in the same way and manner, but with the hands upon the hips, in each of those. Then rise upon the toes and stoop one, two, three times. These done consistently, persistently.

These exercises constantly taken, we will find we will—with the activities of this body—through the other influences that have been given and are being used—make for a change that will make for the greater helpful forces for this body. 877-13

Many of us have a hard time balancing our lives between work and play, for example, or between family and occupations, all of which affects our health. What advice do you have on this concern?

These [conditions] arose as a result of what might be called occupational disturbances; not enough [time] in the sun, not enough of hard work. Plenty of brain work, but the body is supposed to coordinate the spiritual, mental, and physical. He who does not give recreation a place in his life, and the proper tone to each phase— well, he just fools self and will some day...be paying the price. 3352-1

I'm sure that's true, for sometimes we get driven by ambition, not realizing that a different attitude is essential for a better life. But how do we correct such imbalances?

Budget the time, so that the spiritual and mental has its periods of recreation. Budget so that the mental has those relaxations, those periods of stimulation, those periods of social activity that are ever creative. These keep a balance. 257-252

The attitude of the body should be kept in that direction of using the abilities in optimistic and creative thought or activity. These should bring the better conditions for the body. 3195-1

Some people hold down two jobs just to maintain the standard of living they feel they need. Is more than one career advisable?

It isn't [advisable] as careers; it is rather as a working together, a coordinating one [job] with another. When they are made [separate] careers, then they usually become combative one to another— but [they] should be coordinating influences. As the spiritual life of the individual, this may be termed one life; while the material activities may be termed another. But, if they are not made to coordinate *throughout*—and that preached in one direction and not lived in the activities—then sooner or later one or the other must bring destructive forces.

Do not become a crank on any subject! Do not allow self to be led entirely astray, but keep self well-balanced in the material activities, the mental activities and mental abilities, acquainting self with what is *going on* in the material world, the mental world, the social world, and using same—not altogether for self's *at-van-*

tage, but that the body may be, in its abilities in every sense, the better able to serve and manifest—through the activities of self— what it would worship in its inner shrine. 342-1

Western civilization has produced many so-called labor-saving devices, but we seem to be working more hours instead of fewer in order to pay for them.

All work and no play is as bad as all play with no work.... Mentally and physically there should be relaxation for the body for the best mental, physical, and material development. 2597-2

There is more to life than to live, and a success must be one in which the entity may grow in understanding and in knowledge. It must be one in which grace and mercy and truth *have* been and *are* the directing activities; else regrets, in the home, in the associations, may be the part of the entity's experience. Keep self, then, well balanced. Budget your time more.

It is true that one rarely succeeds who has many diversified interests, yet your activities and the dividing of your time should be diversified according to a definite undertaking in a specific direction, that the choice of your dealings with your fellow man may be the more thoroughly understood from *every* direction; and not merely diversified in the attempt to be a piddler in many undertakings. For he that makes material gains at the expense of home or of opportunities and obligations with his own family does so to his own undoing. 1901-1

What else do you recommend for the average person to maintain good health?

Steam or vapor baths—combining witch hazel and the oil of pine, or oil of pine needles and witch hazel [in the steam generator]—will make for purifying, strengthening, cleansing of the body and skin. Such a bath would be taken once a week or, after a bit, once a month, with a thorough rubdown following same, with massage or masseuse activity over the whole of the body. Thus we will find we will keep the body physically fit. 1276-1

More and more people seem to be adopting that advice, for health spas are a rapid growth industry in America today, offering treatments for relaxation and stress reduction. What other benefits do you visualize from a vigorous massage?

Keeps a better coordination between the superficial and deeper circulation.... [When] there have been those tendencies for the activities in the alimentary canal to be choked...this has caused the attempts of the eliminations, through the activity of kidneys, as well as the respiratory and perspiratory system, to attempt to take care of excesses created in the system. This is a tendency, as would be a habit of any form in body forces of an individual entity.

When the sweat baths and the massages are taken, these excesses are eliminated that are never wholly eliminated by the body naturally but are left as part of irritations in portions of the muscular forces, or in the body proper itself. When these are thus eliminated, it also tends—by that stimulation—to turn the correct amount of activity to reduce or to get away from the habit [of poor elimination].

So the cleansing of the colon at times also should be a natural condition, after individuals reach that age to when the activities of the body in a physical exercise are not such as to cause the real activity, slowing the peristaltic movements through alimentary canal. Hence...[massages] are *well* to be taken at times, and also these may be at times taken once or twice a week, then may be skipped for two to three weeks, depending upon the environs, the activity, and what has been the regular activity of the alimentary canal. That is, do not change habits by forming worse habits, but rectify all by keeping body forces coordinating one with the other. 257-252

You mention cleansing of the colon. This may be relevant to the high risk that men face from colon cancer. Is it necessary to cleanse the colon in order to enjoy good health, and if so what do you recommend?

As it is necessary to rinse the mouth, it is necessary to wash the hands, it may be found just as necessary to cleanse the colon. This should be done with enemas when necessary to keep a normal balance, and which prevents accumulations of forces or influences that would cause the excesses which the emotional or general forces of the body itself may not take care of. But let there be an elimination each day through the alimentary canal. This should be taken (such an evacuation or enema) at the temperature of the body, and be sure there are salines or salt in same; teaspoonful to a quart and a half of water, and occasionally a level teaspoonful of soda combined with same. These will *not* produce irritations; these will *not* cause disturbances or prevent the activity of the *natural* influences or forces of elimination but tend to create through the usage of same the strong, *healthy* activity of the walls of the alimentary canal—and to create a better, a more equalized or balanced movement even from the duodenum throughout the entire length of the alimentary canal. 1276-1

The Atomidine[21] taken once, twice, or three times a week—two to three drops in water before the morning meal, not more than this at a time—will also be beneficial. 2831-3

Can anything be done to prevent balding?

A good shampoo with tar soap, and then occasionally massaging into the scalp white Vaseline, will be effective. Occasionally the use, once a month, of such as crude oil is very good. Cleanse this from the hair and scalp with a very small quantity of grain alcohol and lots of water, just enough alcohol to cut it, not enough

21. A commercial product Cayce recommended for such conditions as arthritis and skin problems.

to make the hair itself brittle, then using Vaseline following same. 5165-1

What causes change of hair color and thinning or baldness?

Color of hair and the change comes from the glandular conditions. Age, of course, adds to the disturbance in the glandular conditions, but these are natural causes. And these, of course, may be stimulated or helped with that which adds to the activity of the glands that are exercised in the activity in same—which is a portion of the thyroid; and the addition of foods, vegetables, that carry that stimuli and activity—all those of the iodine content, leaving off the potashes that cause such irritations. 257-252

Is it safe to take vitamins and advertised supplements for restoring gray hair to its natural color?

Safe to take if it is desired—they'll have no effect. 257-252

CHAPTER 6

❧

Financial Advice

MORTON BLUMENTHAL, A New York stockbroker who came to Cayce with an earache, not only got relief—he also got rich on Cayce's business advice. He and his partner on Wall Street were among many business people who sought Cayce's guidance on the bumpy road to financial success. Sometimes, his recommendations were amazingly detailed, such as how to manufacture a hair curling product from persimmon seeds, but more often they were a general prescription for spiritual values in the marketplace and not to cut corners in the heat of competition. His advice proved so successful that Blumenthal and others reciprocated by underwriting a hospital for Cayce at Virginia Beach.[22]

While the stock tips he gave them don't apply in today's market, his words of wisdom on business and financial management

22. *In My Life as a Seer*, Cayce wrote, "For years my great dream was to have a hospital, to have doctors and nurses and the best scientific means of treating people according to the readings. My dream at last was realized." Dedicated in 1928, the Cayce Hospital was devoted to patients who had received medical readings and needed the unorthodox treatments Cayce recommended. After the stock market crash, the hospital closed for lack of financial support in 1931.

have a timeless relevance for those who strive to better themselves financially within a framework of high moral values. Cayce advised not to regard acquiring money as the primary objective of life, but that rewards come to those who provide a reliable service.

Money is often a sensitive topic, particularly among people who have spiritual aspirations and ideals. We want wealth without feeling guilty about it, for many of us have heard the moral admonition that money is the root of all evil. So, how are we to regard this necessity in our daily lives?

First, know what is your ideal—spiritually [such as keeping a charitable spirit], mentally [peace of mind, for example], materially [avoid lavish expenditures]. Know that you must be dependent one upon the other; just as the faith of your fathers is dependent upon the mercy, the love of God the Father; just as the adherence to those principles interpreted in the material relationships brings harmony and peace and prosperity. For, these are one—if they are bound together in brotherly love. 2809-1

For those who like to put their spiritual ideals first, is there nothing wrong with having material ideals as well, such as working hard to provide for our family's material welfare?

It is well to gain that full concept that all there is in materiality is of the spirit; is of the spirit of truth, if it is constructive. They that live by the spirit, through the mental attributes of same, shall prosper in the Lord. They that live by might or main, though their days may be glamorous, find that contentment shall flee away; and those things that make for disorder, disturbance, distrust, must arise in the experience, for these are not the fruits of the spirit. For these [fruits] are they: Just being kind, just being in that manner in which the fellow man is served day by day; and that the outcome of same is fellowship, patience, kindness, gentleness, brotherly love—these manifested in the experience; not by jerks and spurts but as a living example day by day, not to be seen of men alone but rather that which is done in secret shall be proclaimed from the housetops. *These* should be, as has been indicated, the mental attitudes of the body [individual], if there is to be had that which brings harmony, peace, understanding and those things that make not afraid. 391-8

How do you account for those who've become wealthy but appear to be nonspiritual aggressive self-seekers?

To be sure, there may be material successes in sharp practices [shady dealing]; there may be material successes in taking advantage of one another in varied activities; but the Lord thy God is *one*! and this applies in business, in mental, in the spiritual life, and should be construed so—and they that attempt to make them separate do so to their own mental and spiritual undoing, and sooner or later a material and mental failure.[23] 257-182

What are the basic principles for success in business?

To make material success, first make it mentally. For if there are not visions of the help that you give, and knowing and believing in what you are doing, then you have chosen the wrong field. 1537-1

In applying self in any service that is dealing with individuals and things [products] there is required first a thorough knowledge of the subject, or the thing being dealt with, and then it is necessary to work with people in and with the idea that the service rendered [by the business]... will be with the idea and ideal of their building in association with the same [service] what is constructive and in keeping with what will make for *ideals* in their experi-

23. Cayce emphasized that we cannot isolate our business affairs from moral tenets in order to engage in "sharp practices" that might bring monetary success but have deleterious consequences on the soul. The same spiritual laws of God apply in business as well as in personal affairs.

ence....This requires study of human nature, and the needs, wants, desires, in individuals' lives.24

When inspecting or making estimates, then, know the properties [products] that may be in demand, *know* just in looking at individuals who would fit into that picture, to make what in their lives would be a helpfulness in their experience. The associations of business, the work, the people, the returns, the successes for self and for associates, will increase a thousand percent. 912-1

Quite a few cases have come to light lately of business leaders who used questionable practices to gain profits.

Keep your skirts clean! 2886-1

Obviously, one should at least not violate the law on the way to financial success. But how should one conduct oneself in the business world and still allow for spiritual growth?

The question itself is based improperly. For, as has been given, to gain the whole world and lose your own spiritual self or soul is naught. Then, the policies [in business dealings, such as guaranteeing the quality of a product], the activities, in every way and manner, must be in keeping with that which is constructive, that which is active in that way and manner, if there would be a mental, a spiritual, a material success. 257-182

If we accumulate wealth in order to be more charitable, to give larger gifts to our favorite nonprofit causes, is that not a worthy objective or justification?

A laudable one; but do not put the cart before the horse! For, if one cannot render service though his income will barely keep

24. Service to the customer comes first, said Cayce to many clients, and businesses that overlook the customers' needs are doomed because that is poor service.

body and soul together, even if it were tripled or multiplied by a million he would not do any better! Thus, use, practice what you profess to preach. 2409-1

Some investments are risky but seem worthy if the gains allow us to be more charitable.

Don't think you've got to go in to speculate. Don't think you've got to go in and do anything of the kind. Attend to the job that's in hand, and those businesses in hand [that we know to be safe and beneficial], that the things may work on in the proper way and manner; but with the associations and the contacts as will be brought about by the natural association and affiliation...there will be brought those channels and those ways and manners in which the body may make *moneys*, that he may use in whatever way he chooses—but use 'em right! 417-3

Is it necessary to have complete confidence in your business or your product in order to sell it to the public?

Success depends upon how much effort there is and how well *sold* the body (and mind) is upon the associations. To say Yes or No might imply that this is already set. Any choice made by an individual is to be worked *at*. If there is any *question* in the mind of the body as to a service by self being rendered to those whom the body would serve in such an association and capacity, then change. *Do not* continue to sell self on the proposition. Either be sold and stabled in what [is] attempting to be accomplished, or change! 930-2

The entity must first sell the proposition to himself, or no success can be made....That is, no success can be made unless the entity, through its own will force and own volition, is satisfied in its inner self with the conditions surrounding the venture. Then, with that condition, the entity has that capacity to make a financial success of any undertaking, but must first sell self on the proposition. 8-4

What do you say to someone who wonders whether he should get into the stock market to make some money?

That must be determined within self. There is, as seen, in the inner characteristics or basic force of the individual, that [may be] adverse to such conditions, save under certain circumstances or conditions [such as not having a tolerance for risk]. Hence this should be determined within self. 165-5

Many people want to go into business for themselves. What's your advice to them?

The choice [must] be made by self. As to self's abilities, very few there are who may make for themselves a better association than being led or directed with or through associations with others. To be sure, the entity may make a success in business for self; but if self may make for an association in the present that is satisfactory, under the general conditions, remain in that manner. 930-2

If stock trading isn't suitable for everyone, and operating your own business is not always a good idea, is it fair to say we need to know where our talents lie?

Unless you are successful within *yourself*, not in any city or state or foreign field may success come! 969-1

Analyze self, self's faults, and self's shortcomings, and know what *ideals* are in these directions, morally, mentally, spiritually! 1264-2

Why are ideals so important?

[It matters] if the ideal is God, or the purpose for which it entered [is mostly self-serving]. If the ideal is that the entity may have a good time, be well thought of, become wealthy or famous, then these things it may serve. These [objectives], though, it must choose in its application of its abilities. 2981-4

How can an idealistic businessperson survive against competitors who indulge in unfair business practices?

There come periods in your experience when doubts arise as to what brings material success in your experience, and you see about you those [who] disregard law, order, or even the rights of their fellow man—yet from the material angle they *appear* to succeed in gaining more of this world's goods. And they are apparently entrusted with the activities even among their fellow man that will have to do with the lives and activities of many souls. Then you, in your ignorance, proclaim: "What is the use of trying to be good? What is the use of setting a high moral or mental or spiritual standard, when such succeed in entering into the joys of the earth?" They indeed have their reward in that single experience. But have you looked into their hearts and seen the trouble and doubt there? Have you looked into their lives, in their associations with themselves, and seen the fear, the doubt, the shame even often that crouches there? 531-3

Yes, but it is hard to resist the temptation to appear successful and to do what is necessary to achieve it.

True, in a material world material conditions are which individuals or others judge an individual's success; yet [there is] contentment that lies within from a life spent in a service for others—wherein the physical, the mental, the spiritual are treated as a unit, and that all forces work together for good when these are aligned in those of the soul's development....

Choose what would be well spoken of by others for the physical gains, or what will bring content, peace that passes understanding from within, in that hope that may be built in the lives of individuals through the efforts of the entity in those directions that bring for better things. 520-2

That's where free will comes into play, but how does one make that choice?

Rather let the ideal be set in those influences, those conditions that are of the *spiritual* nature, and that there may be used in and through and by self all of those abilities for your own *soul* development, as well as for bringing material success or material gain, or material fame. For what profit it an individual, a person, to have gained the whole world and lost his or her own self respect, lost his or her own association with the Creative Forces—the birthright of every soul as it manifests on the earth! 1193-1

How can we monitor our behavior to avoid compromising such high ideals?

First, then, study within self. Know what are the motivative forces, whether they be prompted by self-preservation, self-glorification, self-indulgences, or by those true influences that the entity will determine in self [to serve the higher ideals], by the grace of the Creative Forces, to make the world—*its* world—a better place for its having lived in same. 1193-1

Aren't we bucking the system when the business world seems to measure success strictly in financial returns, the bottom line?

Use every experience as a stepping stone for success; but *do not* make the mistake to feel that to make a *financial* success is to succeed in the best or the whole matter. While position, power, [and] wealth is to be sought, to be sure—but let these conditions be rather the result from service given in little things, service rendered to the fellow man; for know that he that lends aid in *any* manner with the proper purposes in view—that is, to give self *in* such a service to the fellow man—lends to the Creative Energy [God]. 1720-1

And how should you cope with competitors who indulge in unfair practices to gain an advantage?

Although your contemporary associates in your own fields of endeavor or expressions resort to unfair practices or measures to gain a point or an end, know that these must eventually meet *themselves*—even as your *own* actions must be met. For it *is* the law of love, of hope, of patience, of long-suffering, of kindness, of gentleness, that *will* succeed, that *will* bring its fruit in due season. 1497-1

So you don't think we sacrifice our chances of success by following spiritual ideals?

There is a continual harking to those innate urges for a greater spiritual understanding, that innate call for a greater spiritual awakening. Confuse these not with the material or earthly gains. For the earthly or material gains must be the *outcome*, the *result* of a spiritual, a mental purpose, a desire, an exemplification of same in the dealings and relationships with others, for it to be a permanent or growing experience, and to not become more and more of such a fluctuating nature as to continue to bring greater and greater confusion—until, in the aims and purposes, there is lost the real desire for which the soul sought material manifestations. 1849-2

As a writer, I must confess to often feeling conflicted about the possible financial results when choosing what to write. Some authors are adept at writing "commercial" books that are relatively rewarding financially, while others write what is more rewarding intellectually or spiritually but not financially. How does one resolve this conflict?

If the purpose is first to make money, write differently! If the purpose is first to do good, and the money that should come from same a *result*—this will come![25] 1440-3

25. Few writers make a living as authors, so they support themselves in allied fields such as teaching and newspaper work (Charles Dickens's stories ap-

Some best-selling authors publish a new book so frequently that it appears they do it automatically.

It becomes very poor if you even consider automatic. It *must* be inspirational. You cannot give that which does not shine through what you do!²⁶ 1440-3

Any suggestions for subject matter?

That which in your own experience has been constructive or has brought hope, faith, [and] confidence in that which is Creative. Not that these things belittle the emotions of any form or nature, but let the basic thought ever be constructive. For the world seeks for not what is the easy way but that which is the *surer way* to truth and life and hope. 1440-3

So, basically, when it comes to money you focus your advice on several fundamental principles. What are they?

Do not let prosperity materially undo your mental and spiritual purposes. 2437-1

[Understand the] "give and take" and yet not be moved by reverses or abundance—and here most individuals fail. They may struggle and gain through adversity, but in prosperity fail to give proper values to spiritual, mental, and material things. 2560-1

Learn to use *well* what [is] in hand, then more *may* be *given* you. Remember your talents! 2254-1

Do not belittle, do not hate. For hate *creates*...turmoils and strife. 1537-1

---

peared in the London press before *A Christmas Carol* became a literary classic), but are rewarded by the personal satisfaction that their writing brings. A few write commercial fiction—crime or romance novels—under pen names while striving to publish more serious work.

26. Cayce urged people in all walks of life to let their light shine forth, meaning to show the fruits of the spirit or the Light of God in whatever they did.

Wealth comes from God. This abused, or misused—the individuals *must* pay! For God is not mocked. 2153-10

Would that most people would gain that knowledge that if they are attempting to live a normal life, if wealth is necessary for their soul development, it is a portion of their experience! 498-1

Let business or monetary prosperity be the *outcome* and not the *end* of your endeavors. 5713-1

CHAPTER 7

∽

Dreams Make Sense

CAYCE BELIEVED THAT dreams provide important information for the dreamer who pays close attention and learns to interpret their meaning. This is not a radically new idea, for as long ago as ancient Egypt biblical figures told of dreams forecasting famines and other dire events. But modern science has given little support to the dream message idea.

Sigmund Freud and Carl Jung, however, pioneered serious analysis of the meaning of our noctural adventures. They and several more recent psychoanalysts, such as Erich Fromm, have examined dreams for clues to the dreamer's behavior or emotional state. Cayce cited the value of two main topics addressed by dreams: our physical health, often a warning of a condition that needs attention, and messages beneficial to the dreamer for spiritual or other reasons.

What goes on in the mind when we are asleep?

There are certain definite conditions that take place respecting the physical, the conscious, and the subconscious, as well as spiritual forces of a body. So, in analyzing such a state for a comprehensive understanding, all things pertaining to these various factors must be considered.

With dreams and visions as come to [any] individual, these are of various classes and groups, and are the emanations from the conscious, subconscious, or superconscious, or the combination and correlation of each, depending upon the individual and the personal development of the individual, and are to be used in the lives of such for the betterment of such individual. 39-3

So you think dreams offer guidance for the dreamer?

All visions and dreams are given for the benefit of the individual—if he would but interpret them correctly. For we find that in whatever character they may come, visions, or dreams are the reflection of the physical condition, or of the subconscious. They either relate to the physical body and its action, through the mental or through the elements of the spiritual, or [they are] a projection from the spiritual forces to the subconscious of the individual. And happy may he be that is able to say they have been spoken to through the dream or vision. 294-15

Are dream messages sent to everyone or just to those who are open to such communication?

To every normal body with a developing mind, often those conditions are presented through the subconscious—during the sleeping state—wherein truths are given, visions are seen of things to be warned of and taken advantage of, conditions that will be advantageous to the body, physically, mentally, morally, spiritually, and financially.

Then, these should be taken more cognizance of, that the knowledge (which is power) may be obtained of the truths as to the laws [of God] and conditions regarding the development of an individual body. Hence, pay more attention to the dreams of each and everyone, if the physical forces, the mental elements, the body-mind, the mental attributes, the spiritual development, the moral development, would be such as to make [progress] in a material world. For truths are given, and in this day and age the Spirit of Forces as come from those on High speak as often, through those powers that allow same to be used, as such forces did of old [in ancient Israel, as described in the Bible when Joseph interpreted dreams for the pharaoh, for example]. As these [dream messages] come, then, use them in that way that will bring power, force, strength, understanding, and the peace that comes with the knowledge of the association with those forces that be, that give eternal life here and hereafter. 294-34

Can you give us an overview of the whole sleep-dream activity?

First, we would say, sleep is a shadow of, that intermission in earth's experiences of, that state called death; for the physical consciousness becomes unaware of existent conditions, save as are determined by the attributes of the physical that partake of the attributes of the imaginative or the subconscious and unconscious forces of that same body; that is, in a normal sleep (physical standpoint we are reasoning now) the *senses* are on guard, as it were, so that the auditory forces [hearing] are the more sensitive. The auditory sense being of the attributes or senses that are more universal in aspect.... That is [true] of the lowest to the highest of animate objects or beings. From the lowest of evolution to the highest, or to man.

So, then, we find that there are left what is ordinarily known as four other attributes that are acting independently and coordinatingly in *awareness* for a physical body to be conscious. These, in the state of sleep or repose, or rest, or exhaustion, or induced by any influence from the outside, have become *unaware* of what is taking place about the object so resting.

Then, there is the effect that is had upon the body as to what becomes, then, more aware to those attributes of the body that are not aware of what exists about them, or it. The organs that are known as the inactive, or not necessary for conscious movement, keep right on with their functioning—as the pulsations, the heart beat, the assimilating and excretory system, keep right on functioning; yet there are periods during such a rest when even the heart, the circulation, may be said to be at rest [as they slow down]. 5754-1

What part of us is not functioning when we are asleep?

That known as the sense of perception as related to the physical brain. Hence it may be truly said, by the analogy given, that the auditory sense is subdivided, and there is the act of hearing by feeling, the act of hearing by the sense of smell, the act of hearing by *all* the senses that are independent of the brain centers themselves, but are rather of the lymph centers—or throughout the entire sympathetic system is such an accord as to be more aware, more acute, even though the body-physical and brain-physical *is* at repose, or unaware. 5754-1

You mean that while we sleep we gain a special sense of awareness? How does it work?

The sixth sense, as it may be termed for consideration here, partakes of the accompanying entity [our guardian angel] that is ever on guard before the throne of the Creator itself.[27] 5754-1

What is the sixth sense?

Not the soul, not the conscious mind, not the subconscious mind, not intuition alone, not any of those cosmic forces—but the very force or activity of the soul in its experience through *whatever* has been the experience of that soul itself. See? The same as we

27. The role of angels is discussed in chapter 8.

would say, Is the mind of the body? No! Is the sixth sense, then, the soul? No! No more than the mind is the body! For the soul is the *body* of, or the spiritual essence of, an entity manifested in this material plane. 5754-2

It sounds like the sixth sense is a kind of superawareness apart from our other senses that is informed, as it were, by our guardian angel. What does the sixth sense pick up?

That has to do so much with the entity's activities by those actions that may be brought about by that passing within the sense range of an entity when in repose, that may be called—in their various considerations or phases—experiences of something within that entity, as a dream—that may be either in toto to that which is to happen [a prophetic dream], is happening, or may be only presented in some form that is emblematical—to the body or those that would interpret such. 5754-1

This higher state of awareness you refer to as a sixth sense also sounds like what some people call the higher self, or that part of us that has superior awareness or a keener understanding of what is going on.

This sense that governs such is what may be known as the other self of the entity, or individual. Hence we find there must be some definite line [between them] that may be taken by that other self, and much that then has been accorded—or recorded—as to what may produce certain given effects in the bodies. But as may be seen by all such experimentation, the same effect may be produced upon the same individual, but they do not produce the same effect upon a different individual in the same environment or under the same circumstances. Then, this should lead one to know, to understand, that there is a definite connection between what we have chosen to term the sixth sense, or...the auditory forces of the body-physical, and the other [higher] self within self. 5754-1

What triggers a dream?

Some are produced by suggestions that reach the consciousness of the physical, through various forms and manners as
these. When the physical has laid aside the conscious[ness] in that
region called sleep, or slumber, when those forces through which
the spirit and soul has manifested itself come, and are reenacted
before or through or by this soul and spirit force, when such an
action is of such a nature as to make or bring back impressions to
the conscious mind in the earth or material plane, it is termed a
dream. 3744-5

*Do some bad dreams stem from anxiety or bad habits such as over-
eating?*

There are those [dreams] that are of the purely physical nature—
the reaction of properties taken in the system when digestion is
not in keeping with assimilations, and then one experiences those
conditions that may be called nightmares.[28]

Then there is the mental condition of the body wherein worry,
trouble, or any unusual action of the mind—mentally, physically—[causes] seeking for the way and manner of understanding.
This may bring either the action of the subconscious with the
mental abilities of the body, or it may bring wholly correlations of
material sensuous conditions. These may appear in the form of
visions that are in a manner the key to the situations, or they may
appear in conditions as warnings, taking on conditions that are as
illustrations or experiences.[29]

28. A dreamer told Cayce that he saw himself being served a demitasse when he
    had ordered a large cup of coffee. Cayce said the dreamer's subconscious was
    warning him about taking too much caffeine for his nervous system. Cayce
    himself dreamed of being in church when the floor suddenly caved in. He in-
    terpreted it as a need for a vacation because his work threatened him with a
    physical collapse.

29. A woman dreamed of seeing a beautiful house on fire. Cayce said it was one
    of a series of dreams in which something beautiful was destroyed. The de-

Then there is the action of the purely subconscious forces, given as lessons to the body out of its own experiences. These are phenomena, or experiences for a body to use, to apply, in its everyday walk of life, just as experiences of the mental condition of body may bring the better understanding of conditions to the whole body.[30] 4167-1

If some dreams are trying to tell us something important, like an early warning system, should we write them down in order to remember them and understand them better?

Dreams...may be the correlation of any or all...subconscious direction, capable of using physical faculties and the cosmic and spiritual and superconsicous forces *all* in action, and should be recorded, else the physical in gaining its equilibrium often loses [forgets] much that may be worthwhile to [other] individuals who will apply the same lessons and truths to their individual lives. 294-46

How can we tell which dreams are important?

Depending upon the physical condition of the entity and that which produces or brings the dream to that body's forces. [Some dreams, say of a car breaking down, are vivid in calling attention to an impending physical ailment that needs attention.] The better definition of how the interpretation may be best is this: Correlate those Truths that are enacted in each and every dream that becomes a part of this, or the entity of the individual, and use such to the better developing, ever remembering develop means going toward the higher forces, or the Creator. 3744-5 [Look for a pattern or repeated symbols that may offer insights.]

---

struction represented misunderstanding in her household, which in this dream was symbolic of her ire—a not uncommon dream symbol for anger.

30. A dreamer reported a doctor treated him for a sore toe in a store where people were eating ice cream and candy. Cayce said it was a reminder of the "sore point" in this man's life, which was overindulgence in sweets.

In the normal force of dreams those forces are enacted that may be the foreshadows of condition, with the comparison by soul and spirit forces of the condition in various spheres through which this soul and spirit of the given entity has passed in its evolution to the present sphere.[31] 3744-5

Who can best interpret our dreams for us?

You interpret them yourself. Not by [a] dream book, not by what others say, but dreams are presented in symbols, in signs. Often they may be [the] opposite [of] what is presented to the body, which has been in some of those indicated that bring warnings, blessings. Then keep yourself pure in mind and body. For the Lord's [messages] are often spoken in dreams, in visions. For He is the same yesterday, today, and forever. Be not unmindful that there is the manner of life you live so that you merit this or that experience. 1968-10

With those dreams that come to the entity...the entity may gain the more perfect understanding of the relations between God and man, and of the way in which He, God, manifests Himself through mankind. 900-143

What produces prophetic dreams?

In dreams, visions, and experiences, each individual soul passes through or reviews or sees from a different attitude those experiences of its own activities. And these are, in dreams or visions, emblematical conditions in the experience of that soul-entity[32] 257-136

---

31. Some dreams interpreted by Cayce suggested how to avoid diptheria and polio epidemics.

32. A woman who dreamed of competing with attractive women to hold her husband was told that in a past life she had controlled men with her beauty.

This sort of information gained from our dreams could be useful if we comprehended it and paid attention, is that it?

The dreams, as we see, may be used in the way and manner as have been given, for in vision there is given the correlation of the mental mind with the subconscious forces of the entity, and as the conscious mind only reasons by comparison, and the subconscious by inductive reasoning [drawing general conclusions from a variety of experiences], then the correlation of these are presented in the manner that is often emblematical, often in a way of direct comparison, that entity may gain, through same, necessary lessons for development of mental proclivities of the entity.[33] 137-60

What if we don't remember dreams?

The negligence of its associations...physical, mental, and spiritual. Indicates a very negligible personage! 5754-3

Many people have trouble sleeping soundly, which I imagine interferes with the dream function. What do you suggest to make folks sleep better?

If the body will use a little lemon juice just before retiring, with salt, this will materially aid the body in having better sleep. 816-1

How much sleep does the average person need?

Seven and a half to eight hours should be for *most* bodies. 816-1

What is the main function of sleep other than physical rest and recuperation?

Another woman who was told she had been a warrior leader in a past life had to learn to control her quest for power in this life lest she alienate everyone close to her.

33. Dreams may offer a fresh perspective on familiar circumstances.

Sleep [is] that period when the soul takes stock of what it has acted upon during one rest period to another, making or drawing, as it were, the comparisons that make for Life itself in its *essence*, as for harmony, peace, joy, love, long-suffering, patience, brotherly love, kindness—these are the fruits of the Spirit. Hate, harsh words, unkind thoughts, oppressions and the like, these are the fruits of the Evil forces, or Satan, and the soul either abhors that it has passed, or enters into the joy of its Lord. 5754-2

How is it possible for a conscious mind to dream while the body is asleep?

A conscious mind, while the body is absent, is as one's ability to divide self and do two things at once, as is seen by the activities of the mental mind. The ability to read music and play [an instrument] is using different faculties of the same mind. Different portions of the same consciousness. Then, for one faculty to function while another is functioning in a different direction is not only possible but probable.... *Beautiful*, isn't it? 254-68

What connection is there between the physical or conscious mind and the spiritual body during sleep?

It's ... that *sensing*. With what? That separate sense, or the ability of sleep, that makes for acuteness with those forces in the physical being that are manifest in everything animate. As the unfolding of the rose, the quickening in the womb, of the grain as it buds forth, the awakening in all nature of that which has been set by the divine forces, to make the awareness of its presence in matter, or material things. 5743-3

You once had a client who asked about a dream in which her friend, Emmie, committed suicide. What does that reveal?

This shows to the entity, through this correlation of mental forces of the body-mind itself and those of the body-mind of Emmie, that such conditions had passed through [Emmie's] mind—contemplation of such conditions [suicide], see? 136-54

Fortunately, Emmie did not take her own life. But isn't it an amazing correlation that her friend's dream could obtain this information about what Emmie considered doing?

[It's a] correlation of subconscious minds that contact through thought, for thoughts are deeds and may become crimes or miracles. Just as given in the introduction, as it were, here dreams are the correlation of various phases of the mentality of the individual, see? An individual meaning of that entity.

[In some] dreams...there may be taken into the body-physical elements that produce hallucinations, or the activity of what is induced in the system in itself attempting to take on its individual force produces hallucinations, nightmares....

See how the connection becomes then between the individual mind and that producing same [such as Emmie and her close friend who had the dream]? The same as we find, there may be conditions from the mental mind of an entity, by deep study or thought, wherein the experiences of the individual entity are correlated through the subconscious forces of the entity—the latent forces of the entity—the hidden forces of the entity—and correlating same in a vision or dream. Often these are symbolic conditions, each representing a various phase to the mental development of the entity.

Others there are, a correlation between mentalities or subconscious entities, wherein there has been attained, physically or mentally, a correlation of individual ideas or mental expressions that bring from one subconscious to another those of actual existent conditions, either direct or indirect, to be acted upon or that are ever present, see?

Hence we find visions of the past, visions of the present, visions of the future. For to the subconscious there is no past or future—all [is] present. 136-54

Thus we find latent urges [such as sexual desires] arising in visions, dreams, manifestations.

Have you not wondered why in the sacred writings it is said that God no longer spoke to man in visions or dreams? It is because man fed not his soul, his mind, upon things spiritual; thus closing the avenue or channel through which God might speak with the children of men. For, only they who believe He *is* may make manifest that as a reality in their experience through material sojourns. 1904-2

I see that you had a client who reported having a dream that repeated itself for six years. He visualized an airship heavier than air, which collected its lifting and driving force from the atmosphere by means of points on the top of it. Underneath the machine there were apparently two heavy copper bars running the length of it, having small points underneath, which when charged with the force lifted the machine by neutralizing the force of gravity. The machine was driven by the power streaming from points attached to the rear. What was the interpretation of this dream?

In this vision, we find this emblematical condition being presented to the entity.... As is seen, all of the power must come from above. The bars representing, then, as the individual's foundation, upon which there is given the lifting power of same to soar through the various fields of knowledge in attaining the various points necessary for that development and that understanding to apply such forces in the material plane. 39-3

Good health, we are all taught, requires a good night's sleep. How does sleep benefit the mind and spirit as well as the body?

In purely physical, we find in sleep the body is *relaxed*—and there is little or no tautness within same, and those activities that function through the organs that are under the supervision of the subconscious or unconscious self, through the involuntary activities of an organism [such as breathing]. 5754-1

What does the soul do while we sleep?

Each and every soul leaves the body as it rests in sleep. 853-8

Hugh Lynn Cayce told me that he occasionally experienced astral travel, leaving his body at night while asleep, and looking in on friends in distant places. Do we actually leave the body at times and go to different places?

You do. 853-8

But why?

As to how this may be used constructively, this would be like answering how could one use one's voice for constructive purposes. It is of a same or of a similar import, you see; that is, it is a faculty, it is an experience, it is a development of the self as related to spiritual things, material things, mental things.

Then as to the application of self in those directions for a development of same—it depends upon what is the purpose, what is the desire. Is it purely material? Is it in that attitude, "If or when I am in such and such a position I can perform this or that"? If so, then such expressions are only excuses within self—in any phase of an experience.

For as He has given, it is here a little, there a little—use what you have in hand today, *now,* and when your abilities and activities are such that you may be entrusted with other faculties, other developments, other experiences, they are a part of self. 853-8

How can one develop and use this power constructively?

As to how it may be used: Study to show yourself approved unto God, a workman not ashamed of that you think, of that you do, or of your acts; keeping self unspotted from your own consciousness of your ideal; having the courage to dare to do that you know is in keeping with God's will. 853-8

CHAPTER 8

❧

Beyond God's Other Door

CAYCE TELLS US that death is not the end of life, it is really a new beginning, a new leg on the journey of our immortal soul. From his cosmic vantage point, death is not a fearful experience but the doorway to new opportunities for us to grow and learn and to fulfill our ultimate purpose. Angels are on hand to protect and guide us at every step. Heaven awaits those who love God and their neighbors.

In describing the soul's journey, Cayce lifts our sights above the mundane to catch a glimpse of spiritual realms that await all souls as we approach our destiny.

One of the most mysterious experiences of all is how life as we know it ends. Many of us would rather not think about death, even though we may be closer to that end of our span of years on earth than to the beginning. So, tell us, what is dying like?

Death, as commonly spoken of, is only passing through God's other door. 1472-2 There is no death when the entity, or the real self, is considered; [there is] only a change in consciousness of being able to make application [apply oneself] in the [new] sphere of activity [the afterlife] in which the entity finds [it]self. 2147-1

It is not all of life to live, nor all of death to die—for the beginning of life is as of the spiritual death, unless such life is lived in the spiritual understanding—and the death in the physical is the birth in the spiritual, see? 900-331 Death is but the beginning of another form of phenomenized force on the earth's plane [when the individual's life force is transformed and perpetuated in a mystical nonphysical form we know as spirit], and may not be understood by the third-dimensional mind from third-dimensional analysis [which is a limitation of our experience in the three-dimensional physical environment of life on earth], but must be seen from the fourth-dimensional force as may be experienced by an entity gaining the insight and concept of such phenomenized conditions [on the other side]. 136-18

In other words, we shouldn't expect to fully comprehend death until we are on the other side, in the fourth dimension. Do we awaken to the new reality of the afterlife immediately or how long does it take?

Many an individual has remained in that [state] called death for what you call years without realizing it was dead![34] Passing from the material consciousness to a spiritual or cosmic, or outer consciousness, often an entity or being does not become conscious of what [is] about it; much in the same manner as an entity born into the material plane only becomes conscious gradually [such as an infant slowly becoming aware of its surroundings].... What we see manifested in the material plane is but a shadow of that in the spiritual plane.[35] 5749-3

---

34. Presumably, the individual remained so attached to the material world that it refused to enter fully into the new spiritual realm at hand. Some psychologists, such as Edith Fiore (*The Unquiet Dead*) and William J. Baldwin (*Healing Lost Souls*), believe this explains spirit possession, when spirits inhabit a living human instead of moving on to the unfamiliar spiritual plane.

35. The testimony of many persons who have had near-death experiences, as related to Raymond Moody Jr. (*Life after Loss*), suggests that the Light and the

What about physical desires—for favorite foods, for sex, or for other pleasurable experiences—do they continue on the other side?

When those desires have fastened such [a] hold upon the inner being as to become a portion of the subconsciousness, those desires pass on. Such as one may have in gluttonousness, or in any condition that benumbs the mental forces of the entity. For the subconscious, as given, is the storehouse of every act, thought, or deed—all are weighed in the balance. Hence, the condition as is seen about such entity having passed into the spirit plane; it seeks the gratification of such through the low-minded individuals in an earth plane. For thoughts are deeds and live as such. 900-20

In other words, if we were addicted to certain physical pleasures, and lacking in self-restraint, we may seek to gratify such desires through living persons who are indulging themselves in a similar way, whether it is food, sex, drugs or whatever.[36] Do such cravings haunt spirits very long?

How long it requires to lose physical consciousness depends upon how great are the appetites and desires of a physical body. 1472-2

Aren't we aware of a sudden change once we are free of our physical bodies?

[In most cases] the feelings, the desires for what you call appetites are changed, or [one is] not aware at all. The [in]ability to

---

Love they experienced before returning to their physical bodies was incomparable.

36. An example of addicted spirits is described by George Ritchie, a Richmond, Virginia, psychiatrist who was thought to have died from pneumonia in the army in 1943, but was revived after a revealing out-of-body experience. He writes (*Ordered to Return*) that he saw spirits of deceased people hovering around what you might call "low-minded individuals" in a tavern. Ritchie concluded that it was their attempt to gratify their craving for alcohol, even though they no longer had physical bodies.

communicate [with those on earth] is what usually disturbs or worries others. 1472-2

[Others are] free of the material body but not free of matter; [they are] only changed in form as to matter [no longer confined within a physical body, the entity may nonetheless cling to matter, or the familiar material world due to physical cravings]. 262-86

In the comprehension of no time, no space, no beginning, no end, there may be the glimpse of what simple transition or birth into the material is, as passing through the other door into another consciousness. [In the birth of a child and the death of a person, the soul simply makes a transition, or passes through a doorway, into a different state of consciousness, from the spirit realm to the physical and back again.] 5749-3

Knowing that it happens to everyone, why are we afraid of death?

It is the fear of the unknown. . . . Death is separation and thus man has dreaded it; yet when it has lain aside its phase that makes one afraid, it is but the birth of opportunities. 1776-1

In the separation of the soul and spirit from an earthly abode, each [soul] enters the spirit realm. When the entity has fully completed its separation, it goes to that [assignment] through which the entity merits in the action upon the earth's plane, and in the various spheres, or in the various elements, as has been prepared for its development, so the sojourn is taken, until the entity is ready for again manifesting through the flesh that development attained in the spiritual entity. 294-15

In short, the unknown that we fear is really a series of assigned experiences in the spiritual realm designed for our soul growth, based on our previous progress in the earth. How do you find your way among the various spheres of the afterlife?

Each soul in its walks in the earth has its angel, its gnome, its face before the throne of that which is the First Cause, the

Creative Influence, God. And these are always ready to guide, to guard, if the soul will but put itself in the position in material things [by being open and accepting of guidance] to be guided by spiritual truths. 531-2

It's comforting to know we have an angel for a guide. Is that what is called a guardian angel?
The guardian angel—that is the companion of each soul. 531-2

Do we come under the protection of our guardian angel right after we die, or during our life on earth?
As [the soul] enters into a material experience [as a new born child]—[our angel] is ever an influence for the keeping of that attunement between the creative energies or forces of the soul-entity and health, life, light, and immortality. 531-2

So our angel is with us from the time we are born, and trying to help us fulfill our spiritual purpose?
To each entity, each soul, there is ever the ministering angel before the Throne of Grace, the Throne of God. The ministering angel is the purposefulness, the spirit with which you would do anything in relationship to others. [The spirit in which we relate to other people, whether it be kind and helpful or destructive of such spiritual values, is the criterion for fulfilling our purpose. Our angel tries to protect us from lapsing or backsliding into harmful ways, as it were.] 3357-2

Everyone gains this protection, and no one is left out?
The guardian angel stands before the Throne of God—for each individual. 3189-3

Does our guardian angel do more than protect us?
The guardian angel...is ever an influence...it is a portion of

that influence for *healing* forces. And as may be experienced in
the activities of individuals, [its healing] may become so accentu-
ated as to be the greater influence in their experience. Thus...to
some there is the gift of healing, to some the gift of speech, interpreting of tongues [that is, understanding the meaning of that
state of spiritual ecstasy known as "speaking in tongues"], to ministering. Yet all are of the same Spirit. 1646-1

*So, it is our guardian angel working through us when we display such
unusual gifts. What is the relationship between God and our guardian
angel?*

The guardian influence or angel is ever before the face of the
Father, through [God] may that influence ever speak—but only by
the command of or attunement to that which is your ideal. 1646-1

*As spirits, do we hover over the earth, so to speak, as we sometimes pic-
ture people having an out-of-body experience?*

The spirit of all who have passed from the physical plane remain about the [earth] plane until their development carries them
onward [to other planes of spiritual existence that offer opportunities for soul growth]—or they are returned [to earth] for their development here.[37] 3744-1

What is the nature of spirit?

Spirit is the First Cause, the primary beginning, and the motivative influence—as God is spirit. 262-123

Spirit is...the life itself of the soul, whether in man, in a nation, in a city, in a group, or what. 476-1

---

37. The Cayce readings indicate that the soul decides what it needs as the next
    step in its development, whether it be another physical incarnation on earth
    or a sojourn beyond this realm.

Know that all that materializes must first happen in the spirit. 3412-2

What does the soul look like?

The soul is the God-part in you, the living God. 262-77 [It] was made in the image of our Maker—not the body, no—not the mind, but the soul was in the image of our Creator. 281-41 For while the body changes ... the soul remains ever as one. For it is in the image of the Creator and has its birthright in Him. 1243-1 The soul is the body of, or the spiritual essence of, an entity manifested in this material plane. 5754-2

When the soul departs from a body it has all the form of the [physical] body from which it has passed—yet it is not visible to the carnal mind, unless that mind has been and is attuned to the infinite. Then it appears, in the infinite, as what may be handled, with all the attributes of the physical being. 2533-8

Does the soul ever die?

[It] may be banished from the Maker, not death. 3744-2 For as life is continuous, then the soul finds itself both in eternity and in spirit; in mind, yet in materiality. 1353-1

What is the difference between our soul and spirit?

The spirit is the whole. The soul is the individual. 3357-2

The soul of man is a mere speck in space, yet the soul— though indefinite—is that vital force or activity which is everlasting. Though the earth, though the stars, may pass away; though there may be changes in the universe as to the relative position [of celestial bodies], these are brought about by those combinations of that speck of human activity as relative to the soul's expression in any sphere of experience. 1297-1 The soul is all of what the entity is, has been or may be. 2475-1

Spirit forces are the animation of all life-giving, life-producing forces in animate or inanimate forces. Spiritual elements become corporeal when we speak of the spiritual body in a spiritual entity; then composed of spirit, soul, and superconsciousness.... Spiritual forces being the life, the reproductive principle, the soul, the development principle.... The active principle is the spirit. 900-17

What do you mean by the term entity?
The entity is the soul and the mind and the body of same, see? 1494-1 The soul looks through the eyes of the body—it handles with the emotions of the sense of touch—it may be aware through the factors in every sense. 487-17

The entity is that combination of the physical body throughout all its experiences in or through the earth, in or through the universe, and the reactions that have been built by those various or varied experiences, or the spiritual body of any individual. That which is individual, that which is the sum total of all experience. 262-10

So, Spirit, or God, is found in all Creation—rocks and trees as well as animals and people. What about souls?
Only in man is there the existence of the soul that is not just universal, but individual; capable of becoming as a god, as one with the Creative Forces. 1587-1

Some philosophers consider the human mind our most important feature. For example, René Descartes said, "I think, therefore I am."
The soul is the real self, the continuous self. The mind is the builder, continuous to the extent that it is constructive... and that which is constructive and Good is continuous. 1620-1

What does the mind build?
What is held in the act of mental vision becomes a reality in

the material experience. For [the] mind is the builder and that which we think upon may become crimes or miracles. For thoughts are things and as their currents run through the environs of an entity's experience these become barriers or stepping-stones, dependent upon the manner in which these are laid as it were. For as the mental dwells upon these thoughts, so does it give strength, power to things that do not appear. And thus does indeed there become what is so often given, that faith *is* the evidence of things not seen. 906-3

We tend to think of our bodies as purely physical. Is this not the case?

The body is made up of the physical, the mental, [and] the spiritual. Each have their laws, which work with one another, and the whole is the physical man; yet do not treat physical conditions wholly through spiritual or mental laws and expect them to respond as one. Neither treat spiritual or mental conditions as material, for [the] mind is the builder, and through the mind application of the [universal] laws pertaining to physical, mental, and spiritual [such as cause and effect] one is made one with the whole. 4580-1

While the body is made up of the three divisions—mind and body and spirit—they are one. Yet each interpretation and each application of self, of the entity, of the mental and soul mind, to its experience in the Earth, are just as separate or distinct as may be the application of the body to the elements in the Earth. 601-11

Spirituality, mentality, and the physical being are all one, yet may indeed separate and function one without the other—and one at the expense of the other. Make them cooperative, make them one in their purpose—and we will have a greater activity. 307-10

Most people seem to accept the Darwinian theory of evolution as the way man was created. Is that right or wrong?

Man was made in the beginning, as the ruler over those elements prepared in the earth plane for his needs. When the plane became such as man was capable of being sustained by the forces, and conditions upon the face of the earth plane, man appeared not from that already created, but as the Lord over all that was created; and in man there is found that in the living man, all of that, that may be found without in the whole, whole world or earth plane, and other than that, the *Soul of Man* is what makes him above all animal, vegetable, mineral kingdom of the earth plane.

Man *did not* descend from the monkey, but man has evolved. 3744-4

From what did the human race evolve?

Individuals in the beginning were more of thought forms than individual entities with personalities as seen in the present. 364-10 Those souls that sought material expression pushed themselves into thought forms in the earth . . . they were called the sons of the Earth or the Sons of Man. When the Creative Forces, God, made then the first man—or God-man—he was the beginning of the Sons of God.

Then those souls who entered through a channel made by God—not by thought, not by desire, not by lust, not by things that separated continually—were the Sons of God, the Daughters of God. The Daughters of Men, then, were those who became the channels through which lust knew its activity; and it was in this manner then that the conditions were expressed as given of old, that the Sons of God looked upon the Daughters of Men and saw that they were fair, and *lusted*! 262-119

Evolution, as science today understands it, transpired over eons of time. Is man's evolution still going on?

In all ages we find this has been the developing—day by day, day by day, or the evolution as we see from those forces as may be

manifested by what man has made [for] himself the gradual im-
provement upon things. 3744-4

Is evolution confined to man's experience in Earth or does it include the
spiritual realm?

The evolution of man in the spiritual plane being one, the evolution of man in flesh being another. Hence, [it is] hard to understand conditions in one plane when viewed from another plane,
without the realization of having experienced that plane. Now evolution in flesh, as is seen, is the passing through the flesh plane
and in the various experiences of man's sojourn in earth, through
his environment as created and made by man, this is called man's
evolution in the earth plane.... In the beginning of man's sojourn
in [the] earth plane, we find [him] under what is termed...the
primitive man....As man applies the laws of which he becomes
conscious, the development of man brings forth those results
merited by that knowledge. As man passes into the spiritual plane
from earthly existence, the development in the spiritual plane becomes the same evolution in spiritual planes as is acquired in the
physical plane; and until man becomes in the spiritual sense the
one-ness with the Creator's forces, as set by the example of the Son
of Man coming in the flesh to the earth plane to manifest in the
flesh the will made one with the Father, passing through the physical plane, passing through the spiritual planes, making *all* one
with the Father. This we find then is evolution: Man's development through man's acquiring man's understanding of spiritual
laws, of earthly laws, of God's laws, and applying same on the earth.
Then truly is it given, "The righteous shall inherit the earth." 900-70

Are evolutionary changes directed by God or by factors on earth?

The theory is, man evolved, or evolution, from First Cause
[God] in creation, and brings forth to meet the needs of the man.
The preparation for the needs of man has gone down many, many

thousands and millions of years, as is known in this plane, for the needs of man in the hundreds and thousands of years to come. Man is man, and God's order of creation, which he represents even as His son, who is the representative of the Father, took on the form of Man, the highest of the creation in the plane, and became to man that element that shows and would show and will show the way, the directing way, the Life, the Water, the Vine, to the everlasting, when guided and kept in that manner and form. 3744-4

Why are there such striking differences in how people have evolved in different parts of the globe?

The needs of those in the north country [are] not the same as those in the torrid region. Hence development comes to meet the needs in the various conditions under which man is placed. He [is] only using those laws that are ever and ever in existence in the plane, as is given in that of relativity, that being the needs from one relation to another. 3744-4

Where does the soul come from, and how does it enter the physical body?

It is already there. "He breathed into him the breath of life, and he became a living soul," as the breath, the ether from the forces as come into the body of the human when born breathes the breath of life, as it becomes a living soul, provided it has reached that developing in the creation where the soul may enter and find the lodging place.

All souls were created in the beginning, and are finding their way back to whence they came. 3744-5

You spoke of the further spiritual development of the soul. What is the best way for the soul to develop or make progress?

In service alone may any soul find advancement or development. 721-1 In giving out you receive. 1650-1 As you give, so is it
given. Only what you have given away do you possess. What you
lose was never yours. What you gain is an opportunity. What you
possess is not yours except as you use it in relationships to others,
to your Maker, to your purpose, to your fellow man. 1387-1

What kind of service?
The greatest service to God is service to His creatures. 254-17
In helping the discouraged you find courage; in helping the weak
you become strong. 1650-1

Are you referring to some sort of sacrificial service?
Service is asked of all men [and women], rather than sacrifice.
In sacrifice there is penance, but grace more greatly abounds to
him who sheds the love of the Father upon those that the body
may contact from day to day. 99-8

How can one best serve humanity?
By filling to the best possible purpose and ability that place,
that niche the body, mind and soul occupy; being the best husband, the best neighbor, the best friend to each and every individual the body meets.... He who is willing to become as naught that
they may serve the better in whatever capacity—as a merchant, be
the best merchant; as a neighbor, the best neighbor; as a friend,
the best friend. 99-8

*Saint Paul rates charity as a great virtue. Does charity count as a ser-
vice that contributes to the advancement of the soul?*
That which we give enriches us, rather than what we receive.
4208-12 What is to be given...shall be prompted by the real heart
of the individual, and not by even a suggestion from others. 3663-1

How much should we give to charity?

Ten percent, as all should. 451-1

Being that generous seems to conflict with admonitions to save up for a rainy day or to provide some security for one's old age?

The earth is the Lord's and the fullness thereof, and they who hoard same—whether it be bread, wood, gold, or what—are only cheating themselves in cheating the Lord. For your brethren are your obligation. For you are your brother's keeper. 3409-1

Of course, money isn't the only thing we can give—many people give as volunteers in hospitals and other service causes.

All that you may ever keep is just what you give away, and what you give away is advice, counsel, manner of life you live yourself. The manner in which you treat your fellow man, your patience, your brotherly love, your kindness, your gentleness. That [which] you give away is all that you may possess in those other realms of consciousness. 5259-1

Getting back to the fear of death, many of us were taught as children that we'd go to Heaven only if we were good—so perhaps there is a fear of judgment left over from our childhood.

There is each day set before us life or death, Good and Evil. We choose because of our natures. If our will were broken, if we were commanded to do this or that, or to become as an automaton, our individuality then would be lost and we would only be as in Him without conscience—*conscience*—consciousness of being one with Him, with the abilities to choose for self. 1567-2

Does God judge us in the end?

The judge will be our own conscience, for conscience is what awakens the mind of the soul. 254-54 Each soul [is] accountable unto its own conscience. 1767-2

If we are left to judge ourselves, will those whose conscience seems less sensitive to right or wrong avoid the consequences of their wrongs?

You cannot go against your own conscience and be at peace with your own conscience, your home, your neighbor, your God! 1901-1 These doubts, these fears that come in your experience are but your own conscience—or the mind of the subconscious self— smiting you. 784-1

How can we tell if we are on the straight and narrow?

Act as your conscience and your heart dictate. 254-87

Where does the soul go when fully developed?

To its Maker. 3744-5

Is there really a Heaven?

Heaven is that place, that awareness where the soul—with all its attributes, its mind, its body—becomes aware of being in the presence of the Creative Forces, or one with it. That is Heaven. 262-88

Is Heaven more a state of consciousness than a place to go?

You'll not be in Heaven if you're not leaning on the arm of someone you have helped. 3352-1 You grow to Heaven, you don't go to Heaven. 3409-1

CHAPTER 9

∞

More Than One Life to Live

CAYCE WAS STUNNED when he first channeled information about a colleague who was said to have been a monk in a previous life. There was no place in his Christian doctrine for such alien ideas as reincarnation. However, in countless readings that he subsequently gave, similar information came through about others, including members of his own family and himself: everyone has more than a single life to live. Cayce not only accepted it as valid information but explained that the spiritual purpose of reincarnation is the further development of our immortal soul on one more leg of its extended journey through the universe.

In telling us that the soul needs further development in order to offer companionship to God, you said that is the soul's destiny—but that we don't have to accomplish it in a single lifetime. Would you explain your understanding of how reincarnation works?

Life and its [numerous] expressions are one. Each soul or entity will and does return, or cycle, as does nature in its manifestations [such as perennial plants] about man; thus leaving, making, or presenting, as it were, those infallible, indelible truths that it—Life—is continuous. And though there may be a few short years in this or that [life] experience, they [the multiple incarnations] are one; the soul, the inner self [that is] being purified, being lifted up, that it may be one with that First Cause, that first purpose for its coming into existence. 938-1

If life is continuous and we have multiple lives on earth, as different personalities, why don't we remember who we were in the past?

You only become aware of this as it becomes necessary for you to make practical application in your [present life] experience. 5231-1 When the necessity arises, as to how, where, and in what direction those opportunities were applied, the entity brings those influences to bear in its relationships to daily problems.[38] 2301-4

Why don't we remember them more often?

The same may be asked as to why there is not the remembering of the time when two and two to [you] the entity became four, or when C A T spelled cat. 2301-4

Well, it is true, when you try to recall details from your childhood, not much is readily accessible. Wouldn't it be constructive if we could witness a documentation of our past lives, like reading our own biography, in the interest of making improvements?

Documentary evidence to the mind of the masses is nil. Only that which produces or makes for experiences [from one lifetime to another] that may make a citizen a better citizen, a father a better father, a mother a better mother, a neighbor a better neighbor, is constructive [for the soul]. 5753-2

38. Through regression therapy, flashback memories of past lives have been extensively researched and reported by Ian Stevenson (*Twenty Cases Suggestive of Reincarnation* and other books) and by Brian L. Weiss (*Many Lives, Many Masters*). Dreams or mystical experiences during meditation have also inspired subjects to accept past lives, gaining a clearer understanding of the circumstances they face in this life.

Is it fair to assume that it may be a blessing to forget some of our mistakes or misdeeds in past lives?

As to the experiences in the earth, these have been many and quite varied. Many of these are not well [that is, useful memories] even to be known to self, and thus have they been blotted from the book of your remembrance, even as He blots them from the book of God's remembrance, if you love one another, if you mete to your fellow man, yes, to your sisters in all walks of experience, that love of which you are capable in your self. For he who has loved much, to that one may much be given. 5231-1

You've given readings for people who asked about their past lives, and you were able to provide a few details. Can you give us an example of what you told client 5231, who is a woman?

The entity was in the French land during those periods when many questions might be asked as to what were the standards of activities and morals of the peoples. Though they used beauty and harmony, music and art, there were the thoughts and activities more for satisfying, gratifying of appetites of the body.

The entity was then in the name Fauchee Bannasten. In the experience the entity gained in knowledge, not too much in understanding; though it gained in its spiritual desires to become aware of that which would bring harmony and peace into and unto the soul, rather that that wearying of the world. 5231-1

Did she have other past lives before that one in France?

Before that we find the entity was in the Holy Land when those [her] peoples were journeying there. The entity was among the Midianites who consorted with the peoples led by Moses and Joshua. There was a reckoning, as others were in authority. Yet the entity . . . gained through that experience, for being spared to journey with the sons of Manasseh into the Holy Land. The name then was Jeluen. 5231-1

How did you connect those former lives with the client's present life and her behavior?

In the experience in the present, from those desires [that she experienced in past lives], comes the longing for the awakening to home, home that gives the expression of rest, a place of peace, and comfort, a place where thanks and blessings may be said; the place where each looks out for the other to make that day, that hour, a little more sacred, a little more peaceful, a little more beautiful, yea, to be appreciated; that thanks may be given to Him on high who will, who does prepare the home. For as He gave, "I go to prepare a place for you that wherever I am ye may be also."

Thus is the home, and they who seek to make those places in the earth called homes, indeed blessed among the sons of men. So the desire of your heart to make a home for those who may have wandered, even may have erred in the eyes of man; yet God knows their hearts, and many of those whom you would aid may come to know, too, the blessings of the Holy One, who honored woman that she might, too, be equal with man in the redemption of man from the wiles of the Devil, or the wiles of him who would cause man or woman to err in any manner.[39] 5231-1

Did she have any other lives?

Before that we find the entity was in the Egyptian land, but the entity was among those peoples who were in the groups returning

---

39. In *Many Lives, Many Masters,* Brian L. Weiss, the head of the psychiatry department at Mount Sinai Medical Center in Miami Beach, Florida, gives an example of Cayce's claim that a person's remembrance of a past life may be relevant to a problem in this life. For example, consider the case of a twenty-seven-year-old patient suffering from anxiety, depression, and phobias. When Weiss used hypnosis to help her remember repressed childhood traumas, she described several of her hitherto unknown eighty-six past lives, as well as philosophical messages channeled from "Master Spirits." Her anxieties and phobias soon disappeared, says Weiss, and she was able to end therapy.

with the priest[40] from banishment. And being purified in the Temple of Sacrifice, the entity sought those activities through the Temple Beautiful; misusing in the beginning the privileges granted but learning later, through the analysis of self, just as she may in the present find, how many promises there are in the holy word [in the Bible] that would apply to your own self. And you will find eventually He will talk, He will walk with you. What greater blessing may be in the life experience of any soul?

Study, then, the scripture, for in them you think you have eternal life. You have, and they are that which testify of the living Christ who may abide in your presence, as you minister to those about you in the nurturing of same, in the knowledge of the risen Lord. 5231-1

Are some people indifferent or even resistant to learning about their past lives because they may not have been very righteous? Or they might have been of the opposite sex or a different race—is that possible?

At times. 136-27

What conditions determine our gender or race when the soul returns in a new body?

As to race, color, or sex, this depends upon that experience necessary for the completion, for the building up of the purposes for which each and every soul manifests in the material experience. For as is generally accepted, and as is in greater part true, the experiences of a soul-entity in materiality, in the three-dimensional sphere of activity, are lessons or studies in that particular phase of the entity's or soul's development.[41] 294-189

---

40. This Egyptian priest, Ra Ta, according to other Cayce trance revelations, was a past life of Cayce himself.

41. Each soul is said to choose those special conditions of its subsequent incarnations that are likely to foster its spiritual development. An example is a

Development for what?

That which the Giver of all Good and perfect gifts gave the expressions in materiality when spirit had entangled itself in matter. Thus that which has been given: The will of the Father is that no soul shall perish, but that *all* shall come to know Him and He is. For God *is*, and seeks that man should worship Him in spirit and in truth, even as He is Spirit, is Truth; not as a condition only but as an experience, as a manifestation.

As love is the [preferred] expression for experiences in life manifested in the earth, so is the experience of the soul in the earth dependent upon that [earth] plane, that experience, as to [determine] its race or color or sex. For if there has been the error in that phase, in that expression, the error must be met. For indeed as has been given, whatsoever you sow, so shall you reap. And these are gathered only in the phases of experience in which the associations, the activities, the relations have been. Thus as there is continuity of life expression, so must it continue. 294-189

When the soul returns to start another physical life cycle on earth, is it matched up with parents whose lives offer challenging conditions or opportunities for soul growth?

It approximates conditions. It does not set. For, the individual entity or soul, given the opportunity, has its own free will to work in or out of those problems presented by that very union. Yet the very union, of course, attracts or brings a channel or an opportunity for the expression of an individual entity. 5749-14

Who chooses our parents?

There is the law of cause and effect. There is the law of attrac-

---

friend of mine whose work with the homeless in Virginia Beach, she believes, is a lesson necessitated by a past life when she was a warrior who destroyed villages, leaving many residents homeless.

tion [that like attracts like]. These [people] are not just the same [in all characteristics], though they may join one to another [connect or become close because of a mutual attraction]. Hence the individual entity, of self, chose—partially—because of there being created the channel through which expression [a choice of parents] might be found. 2170-1

Does the incoming soul necessarily take on some of the parents' karma?
Because of its relative relationship to same [the parents], yes. Otherwise, no. 5749-14

Does the soul itself have an earthly pattern that fits back into the one created by the parents?
Just as indicated, it is relative as one related to another; and because of the union of activities they are brought in the pattern. For in such there is the explanation of universal or divine laws, which are ever one and the same; as indicated in the expression that God moved within Himself and then He didn't change, though did bring to Himself that of His own being made crucified even in the flesh. 5749-14

Are the changes we make from one life to the next cumulative and lasting?
As the tree falls, so does it lie. Then as this entity builds in the present experience, creating that activity, that union, that expression of divine love toward the fellow men, then where that is left off, the period of expression is begun where it may take hold. 294-189

How much time is there between lives?
[Incarnations] do not come at regular, given periods, but more as cycles, dependent upon what the individual, the entity, has

done, or has accomplished through its cycle of the earth's passage through this solar system. 311-2

As to when, it may be perhaps a hundred, two hundred, three hundred, a thousand years as you may count time in the present.[42] 294-189

Your son, Hugh Lynn Cayce, told me that you had a difficult time initially accepting what your own readings said about reincarnation because the Bible makes no mention of reincarnation as such. And yet you were finally able to reconcile these apparent differences. Did you find verification for reincarnation in the Bible?

John. Six to eight. Third to fifth. Then the rest as a whole.[43] 452-6

Many Westerners reject reincarnation. What do you think is the strongest argument against it?

That there is the law of cause and effect in *material* things. But the strongest argument against reincarnation is also, turned over, the strongest argument for it; as in any principle, when reduced to its essence. For the law is set—and it happens! though a soul may will itself *never* to reincarnate, but must burn and burn and burn—or suffer and suffer and suffer! For, the Heaven and Hell is built by the soul! The companionship in God is being one with Him; and the gift of God is being conscious of being one with Him, yet apart from Him—or one with, yet apart from, the Whole. 5753-1

---

42. In cases of accidental deaths at a young age, Cayce said the soul often returns more quickly.

43. The Gospel of John records that Jesus was challenged by the Jews when He said, "Your father Abraham rejoiced to see my day." Abraham lived many years (forty-two generations) before Jesus, they pointed out, to which Jesus replied, "Before Abraham was, I am" (John 8:58). Cayce said that Jesus had several previous lives—as Joseph, Joshua, Jeshua, Melchizedek, and Adam.

The story of Jesus and the man born blind man is the most convincing evidence for me in the Bible, when Jesus is asked whose sins the man is paying for through his blindness, his own or those of his parents. The implication is clear that the disciples who asked Jesus that question believed that the man could be punished by a lifetime of blindness for sins he committed before that, or in a previous incarnation. But what will convince others of reincarnation?

An experience. 956-1

I had a dream or vision in which there was the conversation with [my] mother respecting that idea or thought which has been presented or expressed through the information given many [others]—the return of individual lives; born or reincarnated.

And, as indicated, this is to be a proof to the entity [Cayce] that there is the fact of the rebirth, physically, of an entity or soul; as the mother will, in nine months, as indicated, be reborn in the earth—and where and among those near and dear to the entity.

This, then, is merely the expression that there may be the thought, the study, the meditation upon the many phases or manners in which the Creative Forces—God—works in mysterious ways His wonders to perform among the children of men. 294-196

I read that you once saw yourself in a future lifetime—what was that about?

I had been born again in 2158 A.D. in Nebraska. The sea apparently covered all of the western part of the country, as the city where I lived was on the [sea]coast.[44] The family name was a strange one. At an early age as a child I declared myself to be Edgar Cayce who had lived 200 years before. Scientists, men with

---

44. On other occasions, Cayce predicted dramatic earth changes to come, which is also indicated here if a midwestern state gains a seacoast and New York is destroyed.

long beards, little hair, and thick glasses, were called in to observe me. They decided to visit the places where I said I had been born, lived, and worked, in Kentucky, Alabama, New York, Michigan, and Virginia. Taking me with them, the group of scientists visited these places in a long, cigar-shaped, metal flying ship which moved at high speed. Water covered part of Alabama. Norfolk, VA, had become an immense seaport. New York had been destroyed either by war or an earthquake and was being rebuilt. Industries were scattered over the countryside. Most of the houses were of glass. Many records of my work as Edgar Cayce were discovered and collected. The group returned to Nebraska taking the records with them to study. 294-185

How did you interpret that?

This then is the interpretation. As has been given, "Fear not." Keep the faith; for those that be with you are greater than those that would hinder. Though the very heavens fall, though the earth shall be changed, though the heavens shall pass, the promises in Him are sure and will stand—as in that day—as the proof of your activity in the lives and hearts of those of your fellow man.

For indeed and in truth you know, "As ye do it unto thy fellow man, ye do it unto thy God, to thyself." For, *self* effaced, God may indeed glorify you and make you *stand* as one who is called for a purpose in the dealings, the relationships with your fellow man. Be not unmindful that He is nigh unto you in every trial, in every temptation, and has not willed that you should perish. Make your will then one with His. Be not afraid.

That is the interpretation. That the periods from the material angle as visioned are to come to pass matters not to the soul, but do your duty *today!* *Tomorrow* will care for itself. 294-185

Some people have interpreted that experience to mean that terribly devastating changes lie ahead for the earth. Is that true?

These changes in the earth will come to pass, for the time and times and half times are at an end, and there begin those periods for the readjustments. For how has He given? "The righteous shall inherit the earth." Have you, my brethren, a heritage in the earth? 294-185

Why do you think you had this vision?
The vision was that there might be strength, there might be an understanding that though the moment may appear dark, though there may be periods of misinterpreting of purposes, even *these* will be turned into that which will be the very proof itself in the experiences of the entity and those whom the entity might, whom the entity would in its experience through the earth plane, help; and those to whom the entity might give hope and understanding. 294-185

What other dramatic visions of things to come have you had?
I was in the garden here at work when I heard a noise like the noise of a swarm of bees. When I looked to see where they were, I saw that the noise came from a chariot in the air with four white horses and a driver. I did not see the face of the driver. The experience lasted only a few minutes. I was trying to persuade myself that it was not true, that it was only imagination, when I heard a voice saying, "Look behind you." I looked and beheld a man in armor, with a shield, a helmet, knee guards, a cape but no weapon of any kind. His countenance was like the light; his armor was as silver or aluminum. He raised his hand in salute and said, "The chariot of the Lord and the horsemen thereof." Then he disappeared. I was really weak, not from fright but from awe and wonder. It was a most beautiful experience and I hope I may be worthy of many more. 294-185

What did you make of it?
This was a vision. This is the interpretation: These are em-

blems, these are figures in the experience of the entity, that: As is built in the conscious mind of those about the entity, in the conscious entity itself, if there are not those encouragements from your friend, if there is not a kind word or a smile, you do indeed feel that something is amiss, something is awry!

How well, then, those that have named the Name, those that would know the Lord—*smile!* For what else in God's creation can? In the experience there is shown that there is not only the whole armor of the Lord as a defense, but the chariot of the Lord that would take wings upon time to show, to make you know, that His promises abide.

Be faithful through those periods of oppression, as well as those periods that would soon come when the *material* things of life would be as plenteous in your experience. But keep the whole armor of the Lord that you may stand even as He in that day when temptations of every nature, when trials of every sort, come upon you and your fellow man. For the Lord forgets not those to whom He has given charge, "Feed my sheep, feed my lambs." 294-185

Can you tell more about our spiritual development before and after reincarnation in the earth?

This may be illustrated best in what has been sought through example in the earth. When there was in the beginning a man's advent into the plane known as earth, and it became a living soul, amenable to the laws that govern the plane itself as presented, the Son of Man entered earth as the first man. Hence the Son of Man, the Son of God, the Son of the First Cause, making manifest in a material body.

This was not the first spiritual influence, spiritual body, spiritual manifestation in the earth, but the first man—flesh and blood; the first carnal house, the first amenable body to the laws of the plane in its position in the universe.

FOR THE EARTH IS ONLY AN ATOM IN THE UNIVERSE OF WORLDS! And man's development began through the laws of the generations in the earth; thus the development, retardation, or the alterations in those positions in a material plane. And with error entered what is called death, which is only a transition—or through God's other door—into that realm where the entity has built, in its manifestations as related to the knowledge and activity respecting the law of the universal influence.

Hence the development is through the planes of experience that an entity may become one *with* the First Cause; even as the angels that wait before the throne bring the access of the influence in the experience through the desires and activities of an entity, or being, in whatever state, place or plane of development the entity is passing.

For, in the comprehension of no time, no space, no beginning, no end, there may be the glimpse of what simple transition or birth into the material is; as passing through the other door into another consciousness. 5749-3

In one of your readings, given for yourself, you told of spending some time between past lives in the solar system of Arcturus. Why Arcturus?

Arcturus[45] is what may be called the center of this universe, through which individuals pass and at which period there comes the choice of the individual as to whether it is to return to complete there—that is, in this planetary system, our sun, the earth sun and its planetary system—or to pass on to others. 5749-14

Do you mean our souls travel about the universe between lives?

As an entity passes on, as has been given, from this present— or this solar system, this sun, these forces, it passes through the various spheres—leading first into that central force, through which—known as Arcturus—nearer the Pleiades, in this passage

---

45. Arcturus is the brightest star in the constellation Bootes, which is thirty-six light years from Earth.

about the various spheres—on and on—through the eons of time, as called—or space—which is one in the various spheres of its activity. 311-2

What is the purpose of this space travel?

For in flesh must the entity manifest, and make the will One with the God, or Creative Force, in the universe, and as such development reaches that plane, wherein the development may pass into other spheres and systems, of which our (the earth's) solar system is only a small part; in this, then, is meant the entity must develop in that sphere until it (the entity) has reached that stage wherein it may manifest through the spiritual planes, as would be called from the relation to physical or fleshly plane. 900-25

In other words, the soul develops positively during this astral sojourn, but it has to show that it has made progress through another life in the flesh. Does that mean we finish our cycle of multiple lives on earth?

If it is begun on the earth it must be finished on the earth. The solar system of which the earth is a part is only a portion of the whole. For, as indicated in the number of planets about the earth, they are of one and the same [solar system]—and they are relative one to another [in orbiting about the sun]. It is the [soul's] cycle of the whole [solar] system that is finished, see? 5749-14

Speaking of the planetary system, what do you think of astrology?

Well for everyone to make a study of astrology! 311-10

Astrologers ascribe our behavior and our personal traits with the moment and place where we were born. Is that valid or a decisive factor?

Does the time of birth, the place or kind of environment, have a part in destiny? Do the days or the years, or the numbers, all have their part? Yes, more than that! Yet, as has been given, all these are but signs along the way; they are but omens; they are but the marks that have indicated—for, as given, He has set His mark, and these are signs, not destinies. For the destiny of the mind, of the body, or the soul, is with Him. 262-75

No urge—whether of the material sojourns or of the astrological aspects—surpasses the mental and spiritual abilities of a soul to choose its course that it, the soul and mind, may take. 2533-1

Although astrology is very old, it still meets with skepticism. When did people first employ it?

Many, many thousands, thousands of years ago. The first record is that recorded in Job, who lived before Moses was. 3744-4

Why do you value astrology?

For, as indicated, while many individuals have set about to prove the astrological aspects and astrological survey enable one to determine future as well as the past conditions, these are well to the point where the individual understands that these act upon individuals because of their sojourn or correlation of their associations with the environs through which these are shown, see? 311-10

The individual activity [life of each person] is a thing of itself, see? For, as may be illustrated in [the] life of an individual: It may be said that the line of thought in the present is towards [people today believe] a change [is coming] in the Aries age from the Pisces, or from the [age of] Aquarius, or to those various activities, see? But it doesn't mean that every individual changes, for each individual has its own development. As we look about us we see the various spheroids, spheres, planets, or solar systems, and they have their individual activity. Look at the soul of man and know it may be equal to, or greater; for it must be man's ability to control one of such! Vast study, yes! 311-10

Science acknowledges the influence of the moon on the earth's tides but remains skeptical about planets affecting our lives. Folklore has it, for example, that a full moon impacts some people so emotionally that they become "looney." What's your understanding or belief?

In the beginning, our own plane, the earth, was set in motion. The planning of other planets began the ruling of the destiny of all matters as created, just as the division of waters was ruled and is ruled by the moon in its path about the earth; just so as the higher creation [humankind] as it begun is ruled by its action in conjunction with the planets about the earth. The strongest force used in the destiny of man is the sun first, then the closer planets to the earth, or those that are coming to ascension at the time of the birth of the individual. 3744-4

So, you definitely side with the astrologers in believing the stars exert a power over us?

It is not so much that an entity is influenced because the moon is in Aquarius or the sun in Capricorn or Venus or Mercury...but rather because those positions in the heavens are from the entity having been in that [celestial] sojourn as a soul! This is how the planets have the greater influence in the earth upon the entity, see? 630-2

But let it be understood here, no action of any planet or the phases of the sun, the moon, or any of the heavenly bodies surpass the rule of man's will power, the power given by the Creator of man, in the beginning, when he became a living soul, with the power of choosing for himself. 3744-4

That is a significant departure from the popular belief—or misconception—that we are governed by the stars or the sign under which we were born, isn't it?

The *inclinations* of man are ruled by the planets under which he is born,[46] for the destiny of man lies within the sphere or scope of the planets. 3744-4

46. Personalities differ according to different inclinations—tidy versus messy; bossy versus preferring to be led, and so on—and these innate inclinations

Do the planets have such an influence on everyone?

They have. Just as this earth's forces were set in motion, and about it, those forces that govern the elements, elementary so, of the earth's sphere or plane, and as each comes under the influence of those conditions, the influence is to the individual without regards to the will, which is the developing factor of man, in which such is expressed through the breath of the Creator; and as one's plane of existence is lived out from one sphere [the environs or influence of a planet] to another they come under the influence of those [planets] to which it passes from time to time.

In the sphere of many of the planets within the same solar system, we find they [souls] are banished to certain conditions in developing about the spheres from which they pass, and again and again and again return from one to another until they are prepared to meet the everlasting Creator of our entire universe, of which our system is only a very small part. 3744-4

Are any of the planets, other than the earth, inhabited by human beings or animal life of any kind?

No. 3744-4

But our souls visit some of the planets between incarnations on earth. How does that impact the soul?

Many of the forces of each [planet] are felt more through the experience, by the entity's sojourn upon those planets than by the life that is led other than by will, for will is the factor in the mind of man that must be exercised. The influence from any is from what planet that soul and spirit returns to bring the force to the

---

are traced to the dominant planets in one's astrological chart, Cayce would say, but they can be overcome by will power. Thus, no one need be ruled by the inclinations associated with Scorpio, Aries, Leo, or other signs of the zodiac under which they are born.

earth individual, as it is breathed into the body, from whence did it come? that being the influence.

In the various spheres, then, through which he must pass to attain that which will fit him for the conditions to enter in, and become a part of that Creator, just as an individual is a part of the creation now. In this manner we see there is the influence of the planets upon an individual, for all must come under that influence, though one may pass from one plane to another without going through all stages of the condition, for only upon the earth plane at present do we find man is flesh and blood, but upon others do we find those of his own making in the preparation of his own development.[47]

Just in that manner is the way shown how man may escape from all of the fiery darts of the wicked one, for it is self, and selfishness, that would damn the individual soul unto one or the other of those forces that bring about the change that must be in those that willfully wrong his Maker. It is not what man does or leaves undone, but rather that indifference toward the creation [God] that makes or loses for the individual entity. Then, let's be up and doing—doing—"be ye doers [of the word], and not hearers only" [James 1:22]. 3744-4

Is it useful for us to study the effects of the planets on our lives in order to better understand our tendencies and inclinations, as influenced by the planets?

When studied aright, very, very, very much so. 3744-4

47. While Cayce is not explicit in describing the various spheres of influence through which the soul passes during its cosmic journey, he indicates that each soul takes a course marked out for its special enhancement. Thus, not all souls take the same route but ultimately take the one that will best serve their further development.

CHAPTER 10

❧

Tuning In to Spirits

CAYCE DID NOT ordinarily serve as a medium, but he was very much aware, he reported, of the presence of spirits in the borderland hovering about the material world they had recently departed. Among those who believe that life after death continues in the world of spirits, there is a strong desire to communicate with those on the other side. Spiritualists offer their services to bridge the unseen gap, claiming to receive messages for loved ones still on earth, usually reassuring in content but often cryptic in form. Cayce had suggestions for those wishing to connect directly with a beloved soul.

Many of your followers believe that we here on earth are not physical beings but that we are spiritual beings having a physical experience on earth. How can we tell that we are spiritual when we inhabit these very physical bodies?

Many words have been used in attempting to describe what the spiritual entity of a body is, and what relations this spirit or soul bears with or to the active forces [life force created by God] within a physically normal body. Some have chosen to call this [our spiritual aspect] the cosmic body, and the cosmic body as a sense in the universal consciousness, or that portion of same that is a part of, or that body with which the individual, or man, is clothed in his advent [at birth] into the material plane. 5754-2

In the makeup of the active forces of the physical body, it (the body) is constituted of many, many cells, each with its individual world within itself, controlled by the spirit that is everlasting, and guided by that of the soul, which is a counterpart—or the breath that makes that body individual. And when the [physical] body is changed [dies], and this is the soul body [continuing its journey], the elements as are patterned are of the same. That is, what [was] built by thought and deed [during that incarnation] become the active particles, atoms, that make up that soul body, see? 5756-4

The spiritual dimension of the afterlife remains a huge mystery for most of us. We want to know more because we have loved ones who've passed over, and we would like to communicate with them. Is such communication possible?

When they are in the plane of communication or remain within this sphere, any [one] may be communicated with. There are thousands about us here at present. 3744-1

How do we make contact or get the attention of a specific person such as a deceased mother or father?

If there is desire on the part of those in the spirit, or fourth-dimensional, plane to be communicated with, and the same element of desire is attained from another plane, stratum, sphere, or condition, then such may be done. Hence, it truly may be said that all factors have their influence, desire [being] the ruling one; and the desire must be attuned to the same vibration of the one in another plane, as the radio. 5756-8

You mean that the subconscious of the deceased and that of the person on earth must be in tune for them to communicate, like tuning in a radio broadcast?

This is the illustration, see? Both must be in that attunement and separated from the physical forces [or the distractions of the material world] to become conscious [possibly through prayer or meditation]. 140-10

Is it possible for those who have passed over into the spirit plane to communicate at all times with those in the earth plane?

Yes and no, for these conditions are as described—that the *necessary* way or mode must be prepared [like tuning a radio to a desired station]....Those in the astral plane are not always ready. Those in the physical plane are not always ready. 5756-4

Why are we unprepared?

The *mind!* 5756-4

What should an individual do to be ready to communicate with those in the spirit plane?

Lay aside the carnal or sensuous mind and desire that those who would use that mentality, that soul, for its vehicle of expression, do so in the manner chosen by that soul; for some communicate in act, in sight, in movement, in voice, in writing, in drawing, in speaking, and in the various forces as are manifest— for [life] force is *one* force. 5756-4

Does communication require as much effort on the part of the spirit as that made by a person in the physical realm? And can one force such a contact?

Force should never be applied, and may never be applied and be real, in either case. The willingness and the desire from both is necessary for the perfect communication, see? Illustrate this

same condition by that physical condition as is seen in attunement of either [a] radio, or . . . phone, or . . . any vibratory force as is
set by the electron in the material plane. [It is] necessary for the
perfect union that each be in accord. In other words, we find
many in the astral plane *seeking* to give force active [make themselves known] in the material. Many in the material *seeking* to
delve into the astral. They must be made one, would they bring
the better. 5756-4

How have people successfully contacted spirits?

Questions and answers are often confusing, by those that give
or supply information concerning such experiences; for each experience is as individual as the individual that receives same, or
the entity that transmits same, and the possibility, probability, the
ability, of individuals to so communicate, or so draw on those
forces, is raised, limited, or gained, by the act of the individual seeking its ability to so [do]. . . . We find individuals [in life on earth] at
times communicative. At other times uncommunicative. There
are moods, and there are moods. There are conditions in which
such conditions are easily attained. There are others that are hard,
as it were, to meet or cope with [in this life]. The same condition
remains in that distant sphere [the borderland], as felt by many,
when it is the same sphere, *unless* the individual, or the entity, has
passed on [deceased]. 5756-4

*One hears accounts of spirit communication that are disappointingly
brief, such as a child who has just passed into the spirit world and is
able, through a medium to communicate to his mother, "All is well. Do
not grieve. I'm okay."*

Such [a brief message] seems to be in the nature of rebuke to a
sensuous mind when momentous questions might be propounded,
could be, or would be—as some mind would say—given. Remember the pattern is set before. Is the greeting of some pro-

found questions the first meeting? Rather cultivate that of such communications, and receive the answer to that of the most profound that may be propounded in any way and manner to those seeking such information. Is such information always true? Always true, so far as the individual has brought self into that attunement as is necessary for the perfect understanding of same. Do not attempt to govern information, or judge information, by the incorrect law [such as an expectation for more details]. 5756-4

So, we shouldn't be disappointed if we can't have a long conversation with a loved one on the other side. What do we learn from spirit communication?

Many various forms of the active forces of communicative energies, or of soul forces, as are manifested in the spirit world and in the material world...give each and everyone that knowledge that the physical world, and the cosmic world, or the astral world, are one—for the consciousness, the sensuous-consciousness, is the growth from the subconsciousness into the material world.

The [soul's] growth in the astral world is the growth, or the digesting and the building of that same oneness in the spirit, the conscious, the subconscious, the cosmic, or the astral world. We find, from one to another, individuals—individuals—retained in that oneness, until each is made one in the Great Whole—the Creative Energy of the Universal Forces as are ever manifest in the material plane. 5756-4

Does it help to pray for those who have passed over?

Those who have passed on need the prayers of those who live aright. For the prayers of those who would be righteous in spirit may save many [souls] who have erred, even in the flesh.48 3416-1

---

48. Cayce believed in the power of prayer to heal and that this healing power was not limited to physical conditions on earth but could be used to heal the damaged souls of those who "erred" before passing over.

Pray for the dead. And if we are able to attune to such, there we may help. Though we may not call [them] back to life [on earth], we can point the way. 3657-1

If I prayed for my father, would he know of my prayers?

Do you wish him to? Do you wish to call him back to those disturbing forces, or do you wish the self to be poured out for him that he may be happy? Which is your desire—to satisfy self that you are communicating, or that you are holding him in such a way as to retard? 1786-2

Well, I'd just like to ask him what it's like for him where he is now.

First, let it be understood there is the pattern in the material or physical plane of every condition as exists in the cosmic or spiritual plane, for things spiritual and things material are but those same conditions raised to a different condition of the same element—for all force is as of one force.

In that period when the spirit, or when the soul (best that these be classified, that these be not misunderstood, then, in their relation one to another)[49] is in the material, the body physically composed of the physical body, the mind, and the soul, and the subconscious mind, and the superconscious mind, or the spirit. 5754-6

If our thoughts contribute to the makeup of our soul, maybe René Descartes had it right when he said, "I think, therefore I am." Can you describe the soul's composition?

When the soul passes, then, from the physical body, it (the soul body) [is] then constituted with those atoms of thought (that are mind) and are a part of the Creative Forces.... The occupancy [of

49. The distinction between soul and spirit, as offered by Cayce, is that the soul is the immortal part of us, created in the image of God but shaped and developed by our thoughts and acts, and the spirit is the overarching God force in all of life, in the physical and spiritual realms.

their spiritual habitat] is at once—as is seen here, there are about us many, many, many soul bodies; those upon whom the thought of an individual, the whole being of an individual is attracted to, by that element of thought—just the same as the action in the material body—for remember, we are patterned one as of another.[50]

In the next [life, or afterlife], then, we find that what was *built* by that soul is the residence of that soul [whether it be heavenly or hellish], the companion with what has been built by that soul—either of the earthbound or of that element or sphere, or plane, that has its attraction through what [was] created in that soul being in the actions, by the thoughts, of that individual.

Hence we find there are presented the same conditions in the astral or cosmic world [entire universe], or cosmic consciousness, as is present in the material plane—until the consciousness of that soul has reached that development wherein such a soul is raised [through the process of steady spiritual growth based on service to others] to that consciousness *above* the earth's sphere, or [the] earth's attractive forces—until it reaches up, up, outward, until included in the *all*, see? 5756-4

Are those passing into the spiritual plane conscious of both the material and the spiritual plane?

Many carnal minds have passed [over] from the body for days before they realized they were passed. Sensuousness![51] 5756-4

50. Cayce periodically referred to the spirits he could see in the room, as here he says "there are about us many, many, many soul bodies." They are examples, he said of the souls and subconscious minds, fused together and shaped in effect by the thoughts and deeds of the deceased individuals from which they separated at death.

51. Those who have experienced a rich spiritual life through prayer, meditation, and devotions, Cayce said, are better prepared to depart this physical realm for the spiritual world than those who limited their life to sensuous experiences and are so attached to the material world they hover about it instead of moving ahead on their soul's journey.

What is the spirit conscious of?

The subconscious consciousness, as known in the material plane, or the acts and deeds, and thoughts, done in the [physical] body, are ever present before that being. 5756-4

What empowers spiritual beings?

How does the force or power transmitted from the power-house light each individual globe in the city? Each has their connection. Each their various forms, or their various powers, according to what has been set. Now, applying same in the illustrative forces, we find each being in accord, each being in the direct connection, each apply, manifest, according to what is built in the individual in its transition, or in its experience [on the soul's journey], and as the various forces are manifested each give off what is taken on [or gained along the way]. 5756-4

What powers does the spirit entity have?

Raised to the highest power as is developed in that plane, and as *varying* as [an] individual's power or ability to manifest, or to exercise that manifestation, in the material. We have not changed, see? For as we would say: What is the power of an individual in the *physical* plane? Naught as it enters. Naught until it reaches that ability to *give* of self in service. Yet, as we find, there is in all the world nothing that offers so much possibility as when the body of the human is born into the material plane. In the minds of every other, nothing offers more beautiful condition, raised to its same power, as the birth into the astral plane. 5756-4

CHAPTER 11

∽

Jesus, the Man and the Christ

CAYCE LOVED JESUS, as most devout Christians do. And Cayce was devout to the extent that he read the Bible constantly—indeed, he read it from cover to cover every year. Unlike many Christians, however, he did not think Christianity was the only path to God. Those of other religious persuasions should be strong in their faiths, he held. He seemed to consider the various religions like so many spokes of a wheel—the nearer they got to the hub, God, the closer they were to one another; and the farther apart they were, the farther from God.

Jesus loomed large in the Cayce philosophy as a kind of super role model, or "pattern" as he put it, because Jesus embodied what we each should aspire to become in order to fulfill our destiny as companions with God.

What is your view of Jesus—a remarkable mortal or divine?

The Christ child was born into the earth as man; one born in due season, in due time, in man's spiritual evolution, that man might have a pattern of the personality and the individuality of God Himself. 5758-1

Jesus is the man—the activity, the mind, the relationships that He bore to others. He was mindful of friends, He was sociable, He was loving, He was kind, He was gentle. He grew faint, He grew weak—and yet gained that strength that He has promised, in becoming the Christ, by fulfilling and overcoming the world! We are made strong—in body, in mind, in soul, and [in] purpose—by that power in Christ. 2533-7

As the Christ, He was more than mortal man—what was He?

Your Brother, your Guide, your Savior! For He took upon Himself the burden of all. And as you read, as you interpret the 14th, 15th, 16th and 17th [chapters] of [the Gospel of] John, know that these are to you—not to just anyone, but to *all*—"whosoever loveth me and keepeth my commandments, to him will I come—and I will abide with him." 1662-1

Christ [is] that universal consciousness of love that we see manifested in those who have forgotten self but—*as* Jesus—give themselves that others may know the truth. 1376-1 The *power* [to perform miracles, for example] then, is in the Christ. The *pattern* [for how to live] is in Jesus. 2533-7

So, Jesus was both divine and a remarkable human being. The Bible tells little of the early years of His life before He began His ministry. Can you fill in any missing pieces? For example, there are stories told of Him traveling to other lands.

As seen from the records that were kept then[52] regarding the promises and their fulfillments in many lands, "Thou Bethlehem of Judah—the birth place of the Great Initiate, the Holy One, the

52. Cayce may refer to the New Testament records that tell much of the life story of Jesus, or he may mean the Akashic Records, or the so-called Hall of Records, the metaphor for the mystical source he accessed while in a trance to gain information about individuals' past lives.

Son of Man, the Accepted One of the Father." During those periods [Jesus lived] in accordance with those laws and rulings, in the
household of the father.

Then in the care and ministry from the period of the visit to
Jerusalem, in first India, then Persia, then Egypt; for "My son
shall be called from Egypt." Then a portion of the sojourn with the
forerunner that was first proclaimed in the region about Jordan;
and then the return to Capernaum, the city of the beginning of
the ministry. Then in Canaan and Galilee. 5749-2

His first journey took Him to India. How long did this take?

From [age] thirteen to sixteen. One year in travel and in Persia;
the greater portion being in Egypt. In this, the greater part will be
seen in the records that are set in the pyramids there; for *here*
were the initiates taught. 5749-2

What was He taught?

Those cleansings of the body [for purification] as related to
preparation for strength in the physical, as well as in the mental
man. In the travels and in Persia, the unison of forces related to
those teachings of that given in those of Zu and Ra. In Egypt, that
which had been the basis of all the teachings in those of the temple,[53] and the after actions of the crucifying of self in relationships
to ideals that made for the abilities of carrying on that called to be
done.

In considering the physical life of any of the teachers, these
should not be looked upon by students as unnatural conditions.

---

53. The history of Egypt is much older than Egyptologists believe, according to
   Cayce, who dates an ancient regime that built the pyramids around 10,500
   B.C. and used the temple for religious rites and to purify people of nonspiritual attributes. He, and many of the people attracted to him, were identified
   as having been together in that time and place.

Rather as, that the righteous Father *calling* to those that had built in their experience that enabling them to *become* what each individual must in their own little sphere, gradually enlarging same to become inclusive until they—the individuals—are one in purpose, one in aim, one in ideal, with Him. 5749-2

Are there any written records of the teachings Jesus received?

More, rather, of those of the close associates, and those records that are yet to be found of the preparation of the man, of the Christ, in those of the tomb, or those yet to be uncovered in the pyramid.[54] 5749-2

When do you think they may be uncovered?

When there has been sufficient of the reckoning through which the world is passing in the present. 5749-2

You've mentioned the Christ-consciousness. Is that the awareness within each soul, waiting to be awakened, of the soul's oneness with God?

Correct. That's the idea exactly! The Christ-consciousness is a universal consciousness of the Father Spirit. The Jesus consciousness is what man builds as body worship.[55]

In the Christ-consciousness, then, there is the oneness of self, self's desires, self's abilities, made in at-onement with the forces that may bring to pass that which is sought by an individual entity or soul. Hence at that particular period [when embracing the Christ-consciousness] self was in accord [with God]. Hence the

54. Cayce's organization has sponsored archaeological research in Egypt, seeking evidence of an earlier civilization, as well as a Hall of Records believed to be hidden beneath the Sphinx. However, Egyptian government restrictions on excavations near its famous monuments have stymied more than superficial research. No evidence has yet been found.

55. A tendency to worship Jesus among fundamentalist Christian groups.

physical consciousness had the desire to make it an experience of
the whole consciousness of self. Seek this more often. He will
speak with you, for His promises are true—every one of them.
5749-4

How did Jesus become the Christ?

As He applied the law [God's commandments, such as love thy
neighbor]—that is, as Jesus, the man applied the law He made
Himself equal with the law, by becoming the law. No doubt, no
fear, no animosity, no self—but selfless in God's purpose. This
overcomes the law as related to all phases of materiality, including
gravity, including supply, including *all* phases of the experience in
the earth. 2533-7

For as He, your Master, your Lord, your Christ fulfilled the law
by compliance with same, He became the law and thus your
Savior, your Brother, your Christ! For in Him you find, you see the
example that is set before you pertaining to the natural life, the
mental life, the material life, the spiritual life. 1662-1

*Should we think of Jesus as a soul who first went through the cycle of
earthly lives to attain perfection?*

He should be. This is as the man, see? 5749-14

First, in the beginning, of course;[56] and then as Enoch, Melchizedek, in the perfection. Then in the earth of Joseph, Joshua,
Jeshua, Jesus. 5749-14

*Was the life of Jesus, as described in the New Testament, a voluntary
mission for Him after He had been perfected in his previous incarnations and returned to God?*

Correct. 5749-14

---

56. Cayce identified the various incarnations of Adam to include Jesus. 364-7

How can we hope to follow His example when Jesus was such a re-
markable person—on a scale of one to ten, He was way off the end of
the scale—extremely kind and loving, compared to most of us?

[Jesus was] not an extremist, and not a conservative—but one
who met each experience in a manner in which there was *never* a
question in His consciousness as to its purpose, His desire, and
the ability to be one with the purpose of the Creative Forces—
God!

That which has been given may be used to illustrate the difference that may be felt by a soul that has become aware of itself, as
the Christ, or as Jesus the man became aware of the Spirit of the
Father through those experiences of the man as he "went about
doing Good," and at those periods when there was received those
acknowledgments of the Father that he *was* the one who could,
would, through those activities, become the Savior of man. First,
as "in whom I am well pleased"; then as "This is my son; hear ye
him!" 1662-1

To see the spark of God in everyone is the most daunting command-
ment, much less to love them as Jesus did. Is this really possible?

You have not begun to think straight until you are able to see in
the life of those whom you utterly dislike, something you would
worship in your Maker. For each soul-entity in the earth, with life,
whether of this, or that shade or color, or whether this or that dis-
figurement of body or mind, is in the earth by the grace of God.
For He has not willed that any soul should perish, and has thus
prepared a way of escape [from threats of abandonment]. And
you, as His servant, as the child of the living God, are given the
opportunity to contribute to the welfare of any whom you even
consider not quite on par with your opportunity. Thus if you belittle others, what sort of a tree will grow in your own heart? You
may be sure someone else will belittle you. 3752-2

Remembering, as you say, that the immortal soul is the God part of each person may help. If only everyone were more like Jesus it would be easier, wouldn't it?

He *is* the way, the manner in which individuals may become aware of their souls that are in accord with what may be one with the spirit of truth; for corruption inherits not eternal life.[57] The Spirit is the true life. Then, as individuals become aware of that ability *in Him* to be the way, so they become the door, as representatives, as agents, as those that present the way; and the door is thus opened; and not to the man but the spirit of self that bears witness with the spirit of truth through Him that overcame the world, thus putting the world under His feet.

So we, as heirs of the kingdom, as brothers one with Him, may enjoy that privilege He has given to those that hear His voice and put on the whole armor; that we may run the race that is set before us, looking to Him, the author, the giver of light; for in Him you live and move and *have* your being. 262-29

Another more worldly part of me thinks I'm a pretty good citizen—I pay my taxes, give to charity, and observe the law—so why do I need Jesus or religion?

Do you become rebels? Do you find fault one with another, that are as self heirs to that kingdom? Rather be in that humbleness of spirit, that His will "be done on earth as it is in heaven." Thus do we become the children of the Father, the door to the way, and joint heirs with Him in glory.

Let your yeas be yea, your nays be nay. "Let others do as they may, but for me I will serve a *living* God," who has shown in man—*all* men, everywhere—that image of the Creator, in that the

---

57. This apparent contradiction of the theme that all souls are immortal is meant to explain that it is the corruption, or ungodly qualities, that will not survive as the soul evolves in the light and abandons them to be at one with God.

soul may grow in grace, in knowledge, in peace, in harmony, in understanding.

Be you doers of the word; not hearers only. Thus you become the door that the *way*, the Christ, the Savior, may enter in; for *He is* the way, the truth, and the light. 262-29

What do you mean by the expression "He is the light"?

In Him is the life, and He is the light that shines into the dark places, even to the recesses of His own consciousness that casts out fear; for being afraid is the first consciousness of sin's entering in, for he that is made afraid has lost consciousness of self's own heritage with the Son; for we are heirs through Him to that Kingdom that is beyond all that would make afraid, or that would cause a doubt in the heart of any. Through the recesses of the heart, then, search out what would make you afraid, casting out fear, and *He* alone may guide. 243-10

What motivated Jesus to do what He did?

As man found himself out of touch with that complete consciousness of the oneness of God, it became necessary that the will of God, the Father, be made manifested, that a pattern [for humankind] be introduced into man's consciousness. Thus the Son of Man came into the earth, made in the form, the likeness of man; with body, mind, soul. Yet the soul was the Son, the soul was the Light.

The individual entity, then, finds—as it applies that ideal, that life in its experience—a perfect pattern for itself if it will accept it as such; whether as a physical attribute, a mental attribute, or a spiritual attribute. In the acceptance there may be the activity of spirit, activity of soul, activity of the mind, activity of the body. For it is with body and mind that associations or relations are established in the earth, as an entity deals with the physical and mental and spiritual problems of a material experience. 3357-2

There is as much reason to dwell upon the thought from whence the soul came, as it is upon whence the soul goes. For, if the soul is eternal, it always has been—if it is always to be. And that is the basis, or the thought of [the] Creative Forces, or God: He ever was, He ever will be. And individuals, as His children, are a part of that consciousness. And it is for that purpose that He [Jesus] came into the earth; that we, as soul-entities, might know ourselves to be ourselves, and yet one with Him; as He, the Master, the Christ, knew Himself to be Himself and yet one with the Father. 3003-1

What would be a Christ-like attitude?

If the entity will read or study or analyze how the Master treated children, young people, during His ministry in the earth, it will be seen how often He used children, the young people, as the hope of the world, as to how unless each individual puts away those selfish desires which arise and becomes as little children, one may never quite understand the simplicity of Christ's faith; Christ-like faith, Christ-like simplicity, Christ-like forgiveness, Christ-like love, Christ-like helpfulness to others.

In the present, analyze these; and aid in ministering such to the young as a teacher, as an interpreter, as a helper for those of the young who seek to know, to interpret, to apply such in their experience. Yes, even learn how to interpret to children how an individual may pass the collection plate in church on Sunday and swear like a sailor on Monday. Both are of God, one in the right direction, one in the opposite. 1223-9

What is God's will and how do we do it?

"Thou shalt love the Lord with all your heart, your mind, your body—and your neighbor as yourself." This is the whole law—the spiritual law, the mental law, the material law. And as you apply same, thus you become the *law*! For as He, your Master, your Lord, your Christ fulfilled the law by compliance with same, He became the law and thus your Savior, your Brother, your Christ!

Thus as He may act through you in your physical, mental preparation of your body—which has been and is lent to you, yourself, your entity, your soul—you may be the channel. For as He gave, "Inasmuch as ye do it unto the least of these, my children, ye do it unto me." 1662-1

How do we know we are being faithful to His will?

First, patience, love, long-suffering, gentleness, kindness; speaking not of anyone in a resenting manner. For know, as He hath given, all power that is in the influence of an individual, a nation, a country, is only lent of the Lord as an opportunity for the individual according to that it has once purposed—or to carry forward what He has willed respecting each soul! For you know, you understand, all stand as one before Him. There are no ones above another; only those that do His will. 1662-1

Then often in your spiritual meditation, enter into the holy of holies [in prayer or meditation, for example] with Him, for there He hath promised to meet you. For "if ye will open the door, I will enter and sup with thee." This is your promise, this is *yours*— "that ye may be glorified in me," He said, "as I may be glorified in the Father." And thus is the love of the Father for His children fulfilled in your activity.

These do not become then theory—they do not become speculative; but as you do them, so is it measured to you again. For greater love has no man than that he lay down his own self for those that he loves. And that alone that you give, have given—of your body, your mind, your strength—do you possess. Just as He—as your Guide, your Guard, your *hope*—has given Himself; so are you His.

So as you expend your body, your mind, your purposes, your desires, to bring to others the consciousness of His abiding presence, so may you *know* His peace, so it may be yours as you accept, as you use, as you apply same in your relationships to your fellow man day by day. 1662-1

If we make mistakes, as we all do in attempting to follow God's will, are we in danger of suffering some terrible fate, as many Christians appear to believe?

For as He has given, God has not willed that any soul should perish but has with every temptation prepared a way, a manner through which the knowledge of His love, of His promises, may come to the consciousness of His children. . . . And His blessings, His promises *will abide with you* as you abide in His love day by day!

It is not, then, any great influence or force that may be set as to cause the welkin to ring. It is not with the sound of trumpet, nor with the shouting—but rather the still small voice within that brings the assurance to you that you are His and He is yours. 1662-1

Why is it so important to God for us to keep the faith?

So may He—in your work, in your prayer, in your meditation, in your *treatment* of your fellow men day by day—become manifest in their lives. For He increases in power, in might, as you pour Him out in your love for your fellow man by practicing, daily, the fruits of the spirit!

Then not of yourself but that His power of the Christ, working in and through you, may bring not only health but peace—and such peace as He promised; not as the world knows peace but as only those who walk and talk often with their God! 1662-1

Many people may feel ill-suited to serve as God's representatives, in effect.

Well-equipped you may be; putting on then the whole armor of love, of faith, of hope, of charity. Thus may you fill that place, that purpose for which you came into the experience in this earth.

Let love, then, be without dissimulation. Abhor that which is Evil. Cleave to that which is Good—even as He. For He looked not upon men because of their estate but rather "who is my brother? Who is my mother, my father? They that do the will of the Father, the same is my mother, my brother, my sister."

So as you manifest in your dealings with your fellow man the fruits of the Spirit, thus do you become physically, mentally, spiritually equipped for the kingdom of righteousness—which must be within! 1662-1

Our age today seems much more complicated and more threatening than those simpler times in which Jesus lived.

Complex problems arise in the experience of each individual entity.... Are the activities, the relations, ever directed by the spirit of the Pattern [Jesus] that is given to man? That should ever be the question. And the answer can only be as has been given, "My spirit beareth witness with your spirit."

Then, when there are those experiences in the life of an entity in the material plane, when expression is given to that which is the prompting or directing influence in the life of an individual entity, it is ever those that draw nearer to the universal consciousness of the Christ that come closer to the perfect relationship to the Creative Forces or God, the Father—which the man Jesus attained when He gave of Himself to the world, that through Him, by and in Him, each entity might come to know the true relationship with the Father. Thus is the ideal set. Thus should be the prompting of each entity. As to how beautiful this has been and is accomplished oft in the experience of the entity, may not be stressed too much. Yet there is oft within the entity's own consciousness that wonderment as to whether correct choices have been made in dealing with others.

At such times, then, look deep into the life of the man Jesus and see how He dealt with the problems of the day. As He gave, in the interpretation of His purpose in the earth, He recognized the needs of each soul as to its purpose in the earth also. For, all men (and He was a man) have fallen short of the glory of God. Only in Him, through Him, by Him may one attain to that true sonship, that true fellowship, that true relationship to the Creative Forces or God. 3357-2

Jesus said He would come again. When do you expect His second coming?

The time no one knows. Even as He gave, not even the Son Himself. *Only* the Father. Not until His enemies—and the earth— are wholly in subjection to His will, His powers. 5749-2

How do you advise those who wish to get ready for the second coming of Jesus?

In that you seek to know the manner of preparation of Him that would be your guide, seek also to prepare *yourselves* to be His subjects with that same diligence as that which has prompted the seeking here. 5749-2

For there is the continual warring within the individual in every activity as to what it should have done and what it has done about creative energies or the God force in its experience. 1152-1

Yet love manifested, peace exhibited within self, harmony brought by loving associations, makes for opportunities in the physical forces of the life to see demonstrated that which is the basis, the cause, the reason that is the purpose for man's advent, for this entity's advent into materiality; that the love of the Father for His creatures, for His own, may be made manifest in and among those.

For He has given, God has not willed that any soul should perish but has with every temptation prepared a way, a manner of escape for those that will be His own. And as He has given, the will to be, the *will* to make for manifestations of His force and power and love and might has been His gift. So man has the choice. As it is said, there is set before you—before each soul *today*—Good and Evil, life and death. Choose thou. 1152-1

It's usually meant as a compliment when someone is described as "God-fearing." But Jesus would have us believe that God is loving. Should we fear God?

Fear of the Lord is the beginning of Wisdom. Not that fear of disappointment, of contention, of strife, of fault.... If you were condemned by the Christ-consciousness, where would your mind, your thoughts, be? For even as He when they spat upon Him, when they condemned Him, He said not a word; that you might know in His example, in His experience, that you, too, would know suffering, but have a balm in Him; you, too, would know disappointment, but have in Him the fulfilling of all your wishes, all your desires; you, too, would have pain, but in Him have strength and power and might; you, too, would know suffering in body, suffering in mind, but in Him would have strength!

The Wisdom then of the Lord thy God is shown you, is exemplified to you, is *patterned* for you in the life of Jesus of Nazareth, Jesus the Christ! For He indeed in your wisdom is *wisdom* indeed!

How gave He? "If thy brother smite thee, turn the other cheek.

If thy brother seeketh or taketh away thy coat, give him the other also. If he forceth thee to go one mile, go with him twain."

Are these but sayings? Are these but things not understood? Do you say in your heart and your mind, "Yes but He was the Son of the Father and thus had the strength that is not in me"? But you are foolish! For not only are you sons and daughters of the Father but have the strength in the promises of Him who is Life and Light and the Way and the Water and the Understanding! Then the practical application of the Christ-life in your daily experience is Wisdom indeed.

This then is not a thing afar off. Not that you would say as of old, who will bring down from Heaven a message that we may know Wisdom, or who will come from over the sea that we may hear and understand; for Lo, it is in your own heart; it is within your own power, yes within your own might! It is the application of what you *know* to do in the light of the Pattern as set in the Christ. That is Applied Wisdom! 262-104

If Jesus the Christ is the pattern that we are to follow, how can we gain the power to act as He did?

You are chosen, you are sufficient—if you will but apply what you know. For as you apply day by day what you know, then is the next step, the next act, the next experience shown you. Because you have then failed here or there, do not say, "Oh I cannot—I am weak." To be sure you are weak in self, but O you of little faith! For He is your *strength!* That is Wisdom!

Let no one then again ever say "I *cannot.*" It's rather, if you do, saying "I *will* not—I want *my* way." This is foolishness; and you know the Way. For He is Strength, He is Love, He is Patience, He is Knowledge, He is Wisdom. Claim *all* of these, then, *in Him*! For He is in you, and the Father has not desired that any soul should perish but has prepared a way of escape; a way of love, of peace, of harmony for every soul—if you will but claim same, live same, in Him. 262-104

I've read that as a boy you hoped to become a minister but were unable to continue your schooling needed to qualify for the ministry. But hearing your explanation of the significance of Jesus makes me think you achieved your ambition after all.

CHAPTER 12

Good Can Overcome Evil

IN A TIME when many believe that the Devil is a myth, Cayce had no doubt that such a power existed. He explained that just as God is considered the personification of Good, the antithesis is Evil. And what is to blame? Human self-seeking, in violation of the universal laws of God. Man's misuse of free will in rebellion against the Creator has to be transformed into obedience for Good to overcome Evil.

Does Evil exist as a separate force in the world?

Did He not—the Christ, the Maker—say this over and over again? That so long as spite, selfishness, evil desires, evil communications were manifested, they would give the channels through which that spirit called Satan, Devil, Lucifer, Evil One, might work? 262-119

Where did Evil come from?

In the beginning there was the force of attraction and the force that repelled. Hence, in man's consciousness he becomes aware of what is known as the atomic or cellular form of movement....

Yet this very movement that separates the forces in atomic influence is the First Cause, or the manifestation of what [is] called God in the material plane!...

When this First Cause comes into man's experience in the present realm, he [man] becomes confused, in that he appears to have an influence upon this force or power in directing same. [Man thought he held power to create or destroy when ultimate power belonged to the Creator.] Certainly! Much, though, in the manner as the reflection of light in a mirror. For, it is only reflected force that man may have upon those forces that show themselves in the activities, in whatever realm into which man may be delving in the moment. 262-52

Man wanted to feel like he was in charge of the world, I suppose. So, how did he come to terms with the reality?

As man applies himself or uses that of which he becomes conscious in the realm of activity, and gives or places the credit (as would be called) in man's consciousness in the correct sphere or realm he becomes conscious of that union of force with the infinite with the finite force. Hence, in the fruits...of the spirit does man become aware of the infinite penetrating, or interpenetrating the activities of all forces of matter, or what is a manifestation of the realm of the infinite into the finite—and the finite becomes conscious of same. 262-52

What was it like before Evil existed?

In the beginning, [there were] celestial beings. We have first the Son, then the other sons or celestial beings that are given their force and power. Hence that force which rebelled in the unseen forces (or in spirit) that came into activity, was that influence which has been called Satan, the Devil, the Serpent; they are One. That of *rebellion!*

Hence, when man in any activity rebels against the influences of Good he harkens to the influence of Evil rather than the influence of Good. 262-52

Are you saying that man created Evil through misuse of free will?

Will is given to man as he comes into this manifested form [the physical body] that we see in material forces, for the choice. As given, "There is set before thee (man) Good and Evil." Evil is rebellion [against God's will]. 262-52

What was the cause of man's rebellious behavior?

Desire! *Desire!* Hence Desire is the opposite of Will. Will and Desire, one with the Creative Forces of Good, brings all its influence in the realm of activity that makes for what is constructive in the experience of the soul, the mind, the body, one with the spirit of truth....

If the desire of the heart, the soul of self is constructive in your own consciousness, then what you receive in your *own* consciousness may not come save from that sphere, that soul, that may, too, be constructive in its progress through that journey that is before each soul. 5752-3

What was it that man wanted so badly that he rebelled?

The desire to be gods [and dominate his realm], in that rebellion became the order of the mental forces in the soul; and sin entered. 5753-1

Why is the familiar biblical tale of Adam and Eve eating forbidden fruit represented as symbolic of man's rebellion or sin?

It was the eating, the partaking, of knowledge; knowledge without wisdom, or whatever might bring pleasure, satisfaction, gratifying—not of the soul but of the phases of expression in that realm [pleasures of the flesh] in which the manifestation was given. Thus in the three-dimensional phases of consciousness [material world] such manifestations become pleasing to the eye, pleasant to the body appetites. Thus the interpretation of the experience, or of that first awareness of deviation from the divine law, is given in the form of eating of the tree of knowledge. 815-7

In many Christian churches you often hear the term original sin, *as though we are all tainted by sin from birth. Is this true?*

That all have been conceived in sin is only a partial truth; hence often makes a whole lie to those that in the body find their own physical selves may find what their own consciousness they can condemn in another. But to condemn, even as the Master taught when the moral laws, or when the physical laws or spiritual laws were being broken and were presented to Him as examples whereunto they would question Him, He always answered: "Thou hast no power over me save it be given thee from the Father, who has not left His children alone but ever seeks that they should know that the Redeemer liveth." And His light, His life, His love, *cleans* every whit!

And, as He said unto the woman, "Neither do I condemn thee, but sin no more." Neither did He set for her any moral law but that which was conscious within her own soul as to the acts in the physical that would tend to separate or to turn the light into darkness in the life of that soul. And as she came to be known among those that had sought the light, her life became that which led many to an understanding—and still will bring life, light, and comprehension to many. 479-1

What constitutes sin?

It may be defined in one word—disobedience!

In the beginning, the perfect man was given all the attributes of the Father-God, in ideal environments prepared by God for man's material manifestation. Let's draw the comparisons of man-made perfect through experience, and man *willfully* being disobedient.

Self is the only sin; that is, selfishness—and all the others are just a modification of that expression of the ego. But so close is the ego, the I Am, to the Great I AM, that I AM, that the confusions of duty and privilege and opportunity become so enmeshed in the experience of the entity. 1362-1

Sin, then, is willful disobedience. Draw the comparison within yourself as to those experiences indicated in the 1st, 2nd, and 3rd [chapters] of Genesis and those in the 2nd of Luke where we find our pattern, our lesson, and those illustrations that indicate sin versus righteousness, one willfully seeking to know the relationship to the Creator, or the answer, "Know ye not that I must be about my Father's business?" How different from that other, "The *woman* thou gavest me, *she* persuaded me, and I did eat"? 262-125

So in your own self, know that therein lies the spirit of God, the soul of your self. The spirit will quicken, if the soul will but acknowledge His power, His divine right *within* you! Then, let the acts of your body, the temple of your soul, be kept clean in your own consciousness even as the presence of the Master cleansed every body that sought aid from physical dis-ease or corruption and made for the manifesting of the fruits of the spirit, of truth in their lives. Not that it saved the body from the grave, not that it saved a body from its transition from one sphere to another—but *quickened* rather the soul and its mind to such a degree that it would ever cry as did the Master in His message of old to His peoples that had been led through the trials and tribulations, "Others may do as they may, but as for me I—my soul, my body, my mind—will serve the *living* God!" [Joshua 24:15] 479-1

Do we rebel all by ourselves or are we influenced by an Evil force, a Satan?

As there is, then, a personal savior, there is the personal devil. 262-52

What's the best way to resist a personal devil?

Do what is Good, for there has been given in the consciousness of all the fruits of the spirit: Fellowship, kindness, gentleness, patience, long-suffering, love; these be the fruits of the spirit. Against such there is no law. 5752-3

How can we be sure we know the difference between what is Good and what is Evil?

Doubt, fear, avarice, greed, selfishness, self-will; these are the fruits of the evil forces. Against such there *is* a law [of love and truth]. Self-preservation, then, should be in the fruits of the spirit, as you seek through any channel to know more of the path from life—from Good to Good—to life; from death unto life, from Evil unto Good. Seek and you shall find....

Meditate on the fruits of the Spirit in the inner secrets of the consciousness, and the cells in the body become aware of the awakening of the life in their activity through the body. In the mind, the cells of the mind become aware of the life in the spirit. The spirit of life makes [one] not afraid. Then, know the way; for those that seek may find. 5752-3

In the application of these truths, then, we either are aligned with the Creator or not, and we reap what we sow, is that it?

It may be said that, as the man makes in self—through the ability given for man in his activity in a material plane—the will one with the laws of creative influence, we begin with: "Like begets like—as he sows, so shall he reap—as the man thinks in the heart, so is he."

These are all but trite sayings to most of us, even the thinking man; but should the mind of an individual (the finite mind) turn within his own being for the law pertaining to these trite sayings, until the understanding arises, then there is the consciousness in the finite of the infinite moving upon and in the inner self.

So does life in all its force begin in the earth. The moving of the infinite upon the negative force of the finite in the material, or to become a manifested force. 262-52

There are good people who aren't particularly religious, so how does a relationship with God help us?

Seek to know *His* ways. Not alone by denying that sin or error exists. True, sin and error is not of God—save through His sons that *brought* error, through selfishness, into the experience of the souls of men, the body by which angels and archangels are separate from the fullness of the Father. For, in His mercy He has given to all that which is the desire of every heart in a material plane—to seek companionship in a manner that there may be the exchange of experiences in whatsoever sphere the body-soul may find self. And in so doing, if there is the manifestation of greed, avarice, hate, selfishness, unkindliness, ungodliness, it makes for the harkenings that bring their fruit: contention, strife, hate, avarice, and separation from the light. For, those that have turned their face *from* the light of God can only see shadow or darkness and that light is only for those far away.

Yet, if the soul will but turn to the Father of love as manifested in the earth through the Christ, in this life also may there be seen the light and the glory of a *new* birth. 479-1

How can we avoid the various distractions and resist the temptations of the material world that may lead us astray from a spiritual path?

In the material, the mental, and the spiritual experience of many souls, many entities, it has been found that there *be* those influences that *do* have their effect upon the thought of those that would do this or that. Who gives it? Self! Just as it is when an en-

tity, a body, fills its mind (mentally, materially) with those experiences that bespeak of those things that add to the carnal forces of
an experience. Just so does the mind become the builder throughout. And the mental mind, or physical mind, becomes *carnally* directed! 5753-1

*Again, you are saying, it's our choice in what we focus our thoughts
on?*

The mind is the builder ever, whether in the spirit or in the
flesh. If one's mind is filled with those things that bespeak of the
spirit, that one becomes spiritual-minded. As we may find in a
material world: Envy, strife, selfishness, greediness, avarice, are
the children of *Man!* Long-suffering, kindness, brotherly love,
good deeds, are the children of the spirit of Light. Choose you (as
it has ever been given) whom you will serve.

This is not begging the question! As individuals become
abased, or possessed, are their thoughts guided by those in the
borderland [hovering in the spirit world near the earth]? Certainly!
If allowed to be!

But he that looks within is higher, for the spirit knows the
Spirit of its Maker—and the children of same are as given. And,
"My Spirit beareth witness with thy spirit," said He that gives life!
What *is* Life? A manifestation of the First Cause—God! 5753-1

Is Good capable of overcoming Evil?

If the soul were at all periods, all manifestations, to keep in
that perfect accord, or law, with the "over-soul," or the First Cause,
or the Soul from which it comes, then there would be only a continuous at-onement with the First Cause. But when an entity, a
soul, uses a period of manifestation—in whatever realm of consciousness—to its *own indulgencies*, then there is need for the lesson, or for the soul understanding or interpreting, or to become
aware of the error of its way.

Man in his former state, or natural state, or permanent consciousness, *is* soul. Hence in the beginning all were souls of that creation, with the body as of the Creator—of the spirit forces that make manifest in using same in the various phases or experiences of consciousness for the activity.

It has been understood by most of those who have attained to a consciousness of the various presentations of Good and Evil in manifested forms, as we have indicated, that the prince of this world, Satan, Lucifer, the Devil—as a soul—made those necessities, as it were, of the consciousness in materiality; that man might—or that the soul might—become aware of its separation from the God force. Hence the continued warring that is ever present in materiality or in the flesh. 262-89

CHAPTER 13

✐

The Revelation

CAYCE'S UNORTHODOX PHILOSOPHY, while basically Christian with a blend of Eastern mysticism, not only embraces reincarnation but also offers a much more positive interpretation of the final chapter of the Bible, the Revelation of Saint John the Divine, which fundamentalists cite to support their dire theology of tribulation and punishment of nonbelievers. Everyone passes through personal tribulations, not as a penalty for wrongdoing, Cayce tells us, but in the normal course of soul growth on the pathway back to God.

Many different translations of the Bible have appeared since the classic King James Version. Which version offers the nearest to the true meaning of both the New and the Old Testaments?

The nearest true version for the entity is that you apply whatever version you read, in your life. It isn't that you learn from anyone. You only may have the direction. The learning, the teaching is within self. For where has He promised to meet you? Within the temple! Where is that temple? Within! Where is Heaven or earth? Within! Meet the Savior there. For He has promised, "I stand at the door—open. If ye open, I will enter and sup with thee." Again, "If ye will open I will come in—and I and the Father will abide with thee."

There have been many versions…but remember that the whole gospel of Jesus Christ is: "Thou shalt love the Lord thy God with all thy mind, thy heart and thy body; and thy neighbor as thyself." Do this and you shall have eternal life. The rest of the book is trying to describe that. It is the same in any language, in any version. 2072-14

Historians tell us that the books of the New Testament describing the life and teachings of Jesus were written some fifty years after His crucifixion. As a journalist, I know how quickly even eye-witnesses forget details as time passes. How can we have confidence that the accounts by Matthew, Mark, Luke, and John are accurate, especially their direct quotations of Jesus?

For from the very first of the Old Testament to the very last even of Revelation, He is not merely the subject of the book, He is the author in the greater part, having given to man the mind and the purpose for its having been put in print. For it is in Him you live and move and have your being and as He gave, "Search ye the scriptures, for they be they that testify of me, and in them ye *think* ye have eternal life."

If you know Him, you know that in Him you have eternal life. For He is the beginning and the end of all things. 5322-1

Some Christians who believe every word of the Bible to be literally true cite the Book of Revelation as authority for their conviction that the end of the world is fast approaching and that only they, the true believers, will be gathered up into Heaven. Can you shed some light on this part of the scriptures?

The Revelation is a description of, a possibility of, your own consciousness; and not as a historical fact, not as a fancy, but as what your own soul has sought throughout its experiences, through the phases of your abilities, the faculties of your mind and body, the emotions of all of your complex—as it may appear—system.

And you will find *peace*, and an awakening—beautiful! 1473-1

Can you be more specific about the meaning of such figures in Revelation as the various animals and the angels?

Yes, we have the text written in the Revelation, as recorded in the King James Version of same. In making this worth while in the experience of individuals who are seeking for the light, for the revelation that may be theirs as promised in the promises of same, it would be well that there be considered first the conditions which surrounded the writer, the apostle [John] the beloved, the last of those chosen; writing to a persecuted people, many despairing, many fallen away, yet, many seeking to hold to that which had been delivered to them through the efforts and activities of those upon whom the spirit had fallen by the very indwelling and the manifestations that had become the common knowledge of all.

Remember, then, that Peter—chosen as the rock, chosen to open the doors of what is known today as the church—had said to this companion, "I will endeavor to keep thee in remembrance; even after my demise I will return to you" [II Peter 1:15].

[John] the beloved, then, was banished to the isle [Patmos], and was in meditation, in prayer, in communion with those saints who were in that position to see, to comprehend the greater needs of those that would carry on. And, as given in the beginning, "I was in the Spirit on the Lord's day, and beheld, and heard, and saw, and was told to *write*."

If it was divinely inspired, why is Revelation so hard to understand?

[For] the experience of every soul who seeks to know, to walk in, a closer communion with Him. For the visions, the experiences, the names, the churches, the places, the dragons, the cities, all are but emblems of those forces that may war within the individual in its journey through the material, or from the entering into the material manifestation to the entering into the glory, or the awakening in the spirit, in the inter-between, in the borderland, in the shadow.

Hence we find, as the churches are named, they are the forces that are known as the senses, that must be spiritualized by the will of the individual made one in the very activities in a material world. And the elders and the Lamb are the emblems, are the shadows of those acceptances or rejections that are made in the experiences of the individual. 281-16

Why is it presented in the form of symbols?

These are for those that were, or will be, or may become, through the seeking, those initiated into an understanding of the glories that may be theirs if they will but put into work, into activity, what they know in the present. In seeking, then, do individuals find from the beginning that there is presented, in every line, in every form, that good and bad (as termed) that arises from their activity, in what they do about that knowledge they have respecting law, love, mercy, understanding of the wherefore of the Lamb's advent into the world that they, through His example set, may present themselves before that throne even as He, becoming—as given—heirs, joint heirs with Him, as the sons of God, to that *everlasting* glory that may be had in Him.

Then, seek to know what self is lacking...in [your] self? Are you cold? Are you hot? Have you been negligent of the knowledge that is yours? Are you stiff-necked? Are you adulterous in thought, in act, in the very glories that are yours? 281-16

What about the so-called four horsemen of the Apocalypse?

These we see, then, represent *self*; self's body-physical, self's body-mental, self's body-spiritual; with the attributes of the body-physical, attributes of the body-mental, attributes of the body-spiritual, and they are one in you—even as the Father, the Son, and the Holy Spirit is one in Him. 281-16

What does the fall of Babylon mean?

Babylon represented the individual; those periods through which every soul passes in its delving into the varied mysteries that are the experiences of the carnal-mental, the spiritual-mental forces of the body; and, as viewed from that presented, may come to the knowledge only through the *cleansing* that is shown must come to those that would be saved from the destructions that are given there. 281-16

Where are those who have passed on until Christ comes?

As visioned by [John] the beloved, there are those of the saints making intercession always before the throne for those that are passing in and out of the inter-between; even as He, the Christ, is ever in the consciousness of those that are redeemed in Him. The passing in, the passing out, is as but the summer, the fall, the spring; the birth into the interim, the birth into the material. 281-16

In what form will the anti-Christ appear?

In the spirit of that opposed to the spirit of truth. The fruits of the spirit of the Christ are love, joy, obedience, long-suffering, brotherly love, kindness. Against such there is no law. The spirit of hate, the anti-Christ, is contention, strife, fault-finding, lovers of self, lovers of praise. Those are the anti-Christ, and take possession of groups, masses, and show themselves even in the lives of men. 281-16

What are we to think about the belief of some Christians that we will be punished by "tribulation" that is bound to be horrific?

That as built by self; as those emblematical influences are

shown through the experiences of the beloved in that built, that created. For, each soul is a portion of creation—and builds that in a portion of its experience that it, through its physical-mental or spiritual-mental, has built for itself. And each entity's heaven or hell must, through *some* experience, be that which it has built for itself.

Is your hell one that is filled with fire or brimstone? But know, each and every soul is tried by fire; purified, purged; for He, though He were the Son, learned obedience through the things which He suffered. You also are known even as you do, and have done. 281-16

Conservative Christians talk about "the rapture" as though they, the faithful believers, will soon be taken bodily up into Heaven while those who do not subscribe to their belief are left behind to face the tribulation. The rapture appears to be a dubious doctrine originated by an English theologian who gained popularity among American evangelical preachers, even though nowhere in the Bible is there any mention of the word Rapture. *But* tribulation *is mentioned in the Scriptures and some fear for the unfaithful. What does tribulation mean?*

The great tribulation and periods of tribulation, as given, are the experiences of every soul, every entity. They arise from influences created by man through activity in the sphere of any sojourn. Man may become, with the people of the universe, ruler of any of the various spheres through which the soul passes in its experiences. Hence, as the cycles pass, as the cycles are passing, when there *is* come a time, a period of readjusting in the spheres (as well as in the little earth, the little soul)—seek, then, as known, to present self spotless before that throne; even as *all* are commanded to be circumspect, in thought, in act, to that which is held by self as that necessary for the closer walk with Him. In that manner only may each atom (as man is an atom, or corpuscle, in the body of the Father) become a helpmeet with Him in bringing that to pass that all may be one with Him. 281-16

So, tribulation has to do with the hard times we all experience at different stages of our lives. What is meant by the four beasts?

The four destructive influences that make the greater desire for the carnal forces, that rise as the beasts within self to destroy. Even as man, in his desire to make for companionship, brought those elements within self's own experience. These must be met. Even as the dragon represents the one that separated self so far as to fight with, to destroy with, those that would make of themselves a kingdom of their own. 281-16

What is the principal value or message of this book of the Bible?

Former things have passed away, when there is beheld within self that the whole will of the Creator, the Father, the place of abode the forces within and without, make for the *new* heaven, the *new* earth. 281-16

For if you will read the Book of Revelation with the idea of the body as the interpretation, you will understand yourself and learn to really analyze, psychoanalyze, mentally analyze others. But you will have to learn to apply it in self first. For the motivating force in each one of those patterns represented, is that which the individual entity entertains as the ideal. This is the motivating spirit, the motivating purpose. When it is out of attune, or not coordinating with the First Cause, there may not be the greater unfoldment. For, it is in self that it becomes out of attune [out of synch with God]. It loses its power or ability. It loses creative energy or its hold upon the First Cause that is the Creator or God. 4083-1

And in the Revelation study this: Know, as there is given each emblem, each condition, it is representing or presenting to self a study of your own body, with *all* of its emotions, all of its faculties.

All of its physical centers represent experiences through which your own mental and spiritual and physical being pass. For it is indeed the revelation of self. 1173-1

What is meant by the "great city which is called Sodom and Egypt, where also our Lord was crucified"?

Egypt or Sodom or the Crucifixion, or the Lord are conditions, circumstances, experiences, as well as individual places. Then in the minds of those who would attempt or that would seek knowledge, they represent their own experiences. Thus these to the people represent—Egypt, the release from bondage; Gomorrah, as a reckoning with sin—as the Lord was crucified there. As has been given, there has never been an experience when His Christ-mas, His death, His birth, wasn't an experience of the age, the people. Though it may go under many names, as an individual may be under many names, in many environs, there is one—*one* that ever comes as is shown in that later given as to those who have the name in the hand, in the head or in the forehead and the like; that is, what is the intent and purpose. Just as the Savior of the world, as Lord, as Christ—what do these names indicate? That which is a help in a time of trouble alone? Or that to glory in, in your joy, your gladness, your happiness? How many, O how many have there been that have laughed with God, that have wept with Jesus, that have gloried with the Christ! or rather has it been, "My happiness and my joy is of myself"?

No condemnation; but rather is there the pattern pointed to as was set by Him. He was *all* things to *all* men; rejoiced with those that did rejoice; He wept with those that wept. He was glad, He was happy, He was sorry, He kept the faith. 281-33

What is meant by the war in Heaven between the archangel Michael and the Devil?

There is first—as is the spiritual concept—the spiritual rebellion, before it takes mental or physical form. This warring is illustrated there by the war between the Lord of the Way and the Lord of Darkness—or the Lord of Rebellion. 281-33

Are the seven churches symbolic of the seven spiritual centers in the physical body?

Correct. [They are the Gonads—Ephesus; Lyden—Smyrna; Solar Plexus—Pergamos; Thymus—Thyatira; Thyroid—Sardis; Pineal—Philadelphia; Pituitary—Laodicea.] It is well that these are correctly placed, but each individual's *experience* in the application of that gained by each in his or her experience will be different. To give an interpretation that the opening or activity through a certain center raises or means or applies this or that, then would become rote. But know the way, then each may apply same as his or her environment, ability, experience, gives the opportunity. For know, in all and through all, the activity of self is only as a channel—and God giveth the understanding, the increase, to such; and in the manner as is best fitted for the individual. It is not then as a formula, that there are to be certain activities and certain results. These are true in the sense that they each represent or present the opportunity for the opening to the understanding of the individual. For, as has been given, man is free willed. And only when this is entirely given, and actively given to the will of the Father may it be even as the life of the Christ. 281-29

What is meant by the seven lamps of fire burning before the throne, described as the seven spirits of God?

Those influences or forces which in their activity in the natures of man are without, that stand ever before the throne of grace—or God, to become the messengers, the aiders, the destructions of hindrances; as the ways of dividing man's knowledge of or between—Good and Evil. Hence they work ever as those influences that stand between, as it were; being the helpful influences that become as the powers of activity in the very nature or force of man. 281-29

Explain the symbols of the white horse and rider in Revelation 19.

This is the Christ in that it, as the horse, in the experiences of the awakening is the symbol of the messenger; and this is Christ, Jesus, the messenger. 281-37

What is the meaning of 1,000 years that Satan is bound?

[Satan] is banished. That, as there are the activities of the forty and four thousand—in the same manner that the prayer of ten just [men] should save a city, the deeds, the prayers of the faithful will allow that period when the incarnation of those only that are in the Lord shall rule the earth, and the period is a thousand years.

Thus is Satan bound, thus is Satan banished from the earth. The desire to do evil is only of him. And when there are—as the symbols—those only whose desire and purpose of their heart is to glorify the Father, these will be those periods when this shall come to pass. Be *you all determined* within your minds, your hearts, your purposes, to be of that number! 281-37

In Revelation 21:1, what is the meaning of "a new heaven and a new earth: for the first heaven and the first earth were passed away; and there was no more sea"?

Can the mind of man comprehend no desire to sin, no purpose but that the glory of the Son may be manifested in his life? Is this not a new heaven, a new earth? For the former things would have passed away. For as the desires, the purposes, the aims are to bring about the whole change physically, so does it create in the experience of each soul a new vision, a new comprehension. For as has been given, it has not entered the heart of man to know the glories that have been prepared, that are a part of the experiences of those that love *only* the Lord and His ways. 281-37

What is meant by "the new Jerusalem"?

Those then that are come into the new life, the new understanding, the new regeneration, there *is* then the new Jerusalem. For as has been given, the place is not as a place alone but as a condition, as an experience of the soul. Jerusalem has figuratively, symbolically, meant the holy place, the holy city—for there the ark of the covenant, the ark of the covenant in the minds, the hearts, the understandings, the comprehensions of those who have put away earthly desires and become the *new* purposes in their experience, become the new Jerusalem, the new undertakings, the new desires. 281-37

Revelation 22:1 says, "And he showed me a pure river of water of life, clear as crystal proceeding out of the throne of God and of the Lamb." Please interpret this.

As the river, the water, the life represents the active flow of the purpose of the souls of men made pure in same. Then they flow with that purpose from the throne of God Itself, made pure in the blood of the Lamb—which is in Jesus, the Christ, to those who seek to know His ways. 281-37

What is meant by the tree of life with its twelve kinds of fruit that yielded fruit every month and the leaves of the tree for the healing of the nations?

That as the tree planted by the water of life; that is, as the sturdiness of the purpose of the individual in its sureness in the Christ; and the leaves represent the activities that are for the healing of all that the individual activities may contact, even in material life. And that it is *continuous*, as by the month, as for purpose, as for the activities. 281-37

You say it is not known when to expect the Second Coming of Jesus. In what form will He appear?

Then, as that coming into the world in the Second Coming—for He will come again and receive His own, who have prepared themselves through that belief in Him and acting in that manner; for the *spirit* is abroad, and the time draws near, and there will be the reckoning of those even as in the first so in the last, and the last shall be first; for there is that Spirit abroad—He stands near. He that has eyes to see, let him see. He that has ears to hear, let him hear that music of the coming of the Lord of this vineyard, and art *you* ready to give account of what you have done with your opportunity in the earth as the Sons of God, as the heirs and joint heirs of glory *with* the Son? Then make your paths straight, for there must come an answering for what you have done with your Lord! He will not tarry, for having overcome He shall appear even *as* the Lord *and* Master. Not as one born, but as one that returns to His own, for He will walk and talk with men of every clime, and those that are faithful and just in their reckoning shall be caught up with Him to rule and to do *judgment* for a thousand years! 364-7

Will He appear more than one more time?

He will come again and again in the hearts, in the minds, in the experiences of those that *love* His coming. But those when they think on Him and know what His Presence would mean and become fearful, He passes by—even as the experiences of the entity through that sojourn found many that harkened not to the simple words of Him who gave, "Know thyself, know that thy Father abideth in you. And if you love Him, you may know His ways, His experiences." 1152-1

CHAPTER 14

∽

No Soul Is Left Behind

PUNISHMENT AS WE usually think of it is not the fate of errant souls, says Cayce. Instead, we live under the law of karma, which comes into play when we rebel against God or violate such spiritual ideals as love and charity with self-indulgent acts that are harmful to others. Karma obliges us to face ourselves until we repent of such willful behavior and discover that joy is found in union, or at-onement, with our Creator. Karmic debts incurred in one lifetime may be repaid in another incarnation as new circumstances challenge us to rise above past missteps.

With such extended opportunities for soul growth, Cayce assures us that no one is banished from the kingdom of God and no soul is left behind.

We hear more about karma than punishment when it comes to paying for our shortcomings or our sins. What is karma?

That which is cosmic—or destiny, or karma—depends upon what the soul has done about what it has become aware of. "As ye sow, so shall ye reap" (Galatians 6:7). And like begets like.
267-7

Is karma a religious precept or a philosophical principle?

Whether considered philosophy or religion or whether from the scientific manner of cause and effect, karma is all of these and more. 440-5

How does karma work?

Rather it may be likened unto a piece of food, whether fish or bread, taken into the system; it is assimilated by the organs of digestion, and then those elements that are gathered from same [foods] are made into the forces that flow through the body, giving the strength and vitality to an animate object, or being, or body.

So, [it is] in experiences of a soul, in a body, in an experience in the earth. Its [the entity's] thoughts make for what the soul feeds upon, as do the activities that are carried on from [or inspired from] the thought of the period. . . . Then the soul [in a later incarnation] reentering into a body under a different environ either makes for the expending of what it has [previously] made through the experience of the sojourn in a form that is called in some religions destiny of the soul; in another philosophy what has been built must be met in some way or manner; or in the more scientific manner that a certain cause produces a certain effect. Hence, we see that karma is all of these and more. 440-5

In short, our thoughts lead to behavior that in turn affects the soul, for better or for worse. When it's worse, we have a chance to redeem it during a later incarnation. What more is there to karma?

It's what the soul-mind has done about the source of redemption of the soul! Or it may be yet cause and effect, as related to the soul, the mind, the spirit, the body. 440-5

Karma is, then, that which has been in the past built as indifference to what [is] known to be right. Taking chances, as it were—"Will do better tomorrow—this suits my purpose today—I'll do better tomorrow." 257-78

Every harsh word, every unkind thing, no matter what others have done, [or] what an individual says about another individual, must be met by self. For only self can actually defame self. 257-122

How is karma different from cause and effect?

Cause and effect to many are the same as karma. [But] karma is what [is] brought over, while cause and effect may exist in one material experience only. 314-1

In other words, cause-and-effect experiences, such as lung cancer from smoking, end at death, while karmic debts are spiritual in nature, such as betraying a friend, and carry over into the afterlife or from life to later life?

[Karmic] influences are more of the spiritual than of the earth's experience, for what we create in the earth we meet in the earth—and what we create in the realm through spiritual forces we meet there! 314-1

Karmic influence is, then, rebellious influence against [God's will]. When opportunities [for redemption] are presented, it is the entity's own will force that must be exercised [if the healing of a relationship, say, is to be realized]....Hence as for the entity's fulfilling, it is ever on the road. 903-23

Is punishment involved in paying off karmic debts?

It is merely self being met in relationship to what...[we] are working out; and not a karmic debt *between* [us and another person], but a karmic debt *of* self that may be worked out...[through relationships] that exist in the present![58] 1436-3

58. Bruce MacArthur, in *Your Life: Why It Is the Way It Is and What You Can Do about It,* offers an exaggerated example of a man who broke his leg, whose house burned down, and whose wife ran off with his best friend. "A simplified explanation might be that in the past you had broken someone's leg, burned down that individual's house, and run off with his spouse—now you are meeting yourself."

Are there other ways to free ourselves of bad karma?

Karma can be met most in Him who, taking away the law of cause and effect by fulfilling the law, establishes the law of grace. 2828-4

God, then, can wipe out our debts. We often use the expression "by the grace of God" as though recognizing that God might let us off easy. What persuades God to forgive our mistakes?

It is only as *you* forgive [others] that even the Savior, the Christ, is able to forgive you. 3124-2 As you forgive, you are forgiven. As you love, so are you loved. As you resent, so are you resented. This is *law*—physical, mental, and *spiritual!* 2600-2

I guess we need God's mercy, for it seems part of the human condition to resent some things. How can we be sure we will be treated mercifully?

How? As you would have mercy shown you, you show mercy to those that even despitefully [maliciously] use you. If you would be forgiven for that which is contrary to your own purposes [such as hating instead of loving your neighbor]—yet through the vicissitudes of the experiences about you, anger and wrath give place to better judgment—you, too, will forgive those that have despitefully used you; you will hold no malice. For you would that your Ideal, that Way you seek, hold no malice—yea, no judgment—against you. 987-4

You've given us a concept of Heaven as a state of being that results from service to others. What about Hell?

Heaven and Hell are built by the soul! 5753-1 To live in life with a conscience that is continually dogging you, continually warning against your own better self in the desire to do Good, is to indeed live in a hellfire itself. 417-8

Can we save someone from that sort of suffering?

From what may anyone be saved? Only from themselves! That is their individual hell; they dig it with their own desires! 262-40

So it is up to each of us to save ourselves from ending up in hellfire? What makes the difference?

Know yourself first. Look within your own heart. What is it you would purpose to do? Satisfy your own appetites? Satisfy your own desire for power or glory, for fame or fortune? These, as you have experienced and as you know within your deeper self, easily take wings and fly away. Only those things that are just, those things that are beautiful, those things that are harmonious, that arise from brotherly kindness, brotherly love, patience, hope, and graciousness, *live*. These are the fruits of those unseen forces that you recognize as being the powers that rule this universe—yea, this heterogeneous mass of human emotions and human souls; that power which arises from *Good*, not from hate nor malice nor greed nor covetousness. For these take hold upon the gates of Hell and are the torments to man's soul! 1776-1

If we have wronged others, don't we also have to repent? If so, how?

Repentance, then, is, "Not my will but thine, O Lord, be done in me, through me, day by day." 2533-7

How do we know God's will?

The answer to know His way is ever within...and know that attunement, atonement, and at-onement are one. 2174-3

What is at-onement?

At-onement is making self's will one with the Creative Forces, that [it] may become the impelling influence in thought [and] in mind, that is, the builder to every act of a physical, mental, or material body. 262-45

You mean the soul progresses as we align our thoughts and deeds with God. Why did God give us free will if it's God's will that we should follow?

The birthright of every soul is choice, or will. 2329-1 Choice is made by the will, guided by the mental according to what in the consciousness of self is an entity's ideal. 1885-1 Each individual has the choice, which no one has the right to supersede—even God does not! 254-102

But if God wants us to center our lives and beliefs in Him, and we rebel and take another direction, and it becomes a test of wills, it is hard to imagine that our will could stand up to God's. I mean if we go eyeball to eyeball with God, who do you think will blink first?

If our will were broken, if we were commanded to do this or that, or to become as an automaton, our individuality then would be lost and we would only be as in Him without conscience—conscience—consciousness of being one with Him, with the abilities to choose for self. 1567-2

So, God won't force us to comply with His wishes?

Man alone is given . . . free will. He alone may defy God. 5757-1.

No force-feeding spirituality? So what happens if we keep God at arm's length?

Though the heavens fall, though the earth may pass away, in His own time He will draw you—if you but show your willingness to be drawn [to Him], but not against your own better or inner self. 366-5

And yet isn't everyone tempted to make bad choices?

We have continually the conflicting influences, or Good and [Evil], constantly before an entity for choice. For with free will we become as the children of the Father. Without free will we become automatons, or as nature in its beauty—but ever just that expression; while the soul of man may grow to be equal with, one with, the Creative Forces. 1435-1

Why do we have free will if it can cause us so much trouble?

Will is the factor in the experience of each soul making it separate or individual. It is the individuality of the soul. 3351-1 For the will of each entity, of each soul, is what individualizes it, makes it aware of itself. 853-9

And, of course, we can exercise our free will to follow the Good, or God.

The will of the soul attuned to God may change the circumstances of the environment...in fact, all the forces even in nature itself. 3374-1

Everyone's personality is different, some more rebellious or willful than others—is this an expression of the soul?

Personality is what you wish others to think and see. Individuality is what your soul prays, your soul hopes for, desires. 5246-1 The individuality is that with which you live yourself, your inner self. And this is deep, far-reaching....Your personality, then, is the material expression; and your individuality is the personality of the soul. 2995-1

That's a fascinating distinction, that our individuality comes from our soul. What determines whether the soul makes any progress?

Know that it is this will—the birthright of each soul—that makes for growth or retardment in any given experience or activity. 1992-1

But exercising this birthright is often considered rebellion—rebellion against parents initially, or social customs, civil authority, and even against religious teachings. Why is that?

As soon as man contemplates his free will he thinks of it as a means of doing the opposite of God's will, although he finds that only by doing God's will does he find happiness. Yet the notion of serving doesn't sit well with him, for he sees it as a sacrifice of his will. Only in disillusion and suffering, in time, space, and patience, does he come to the wisdom that his real will is the will of God, and its practice is happiness and Heaven. 2537-1

So you believe that sooner or later we all learn this lesson and get right with God?

Can the will of man continue to defy its Maker? 826-8

It sounds like most of us are capable of such defiance, some of us for a lifetime. What happens when we see the light?

The soul, then, must return—*will* return—to its Maker. It is a portion of the Creative Forces, which is energized into activity even in materiality, in the flesh. 272-9

So, we really have no choice?

God Himself knows not what man will decide to do with himself.... He has given man free will. Man destines the body. 262-82

And yet you say it is the destiny of each of us ultimately to become one with God?

Unless the entity wills its [own] banishment. 900-20

Banishment is a scary word. And some Christians are scared to death that they might be banished or denied union with God. They have been taught that only a privileged few will ascend to a heavenly reward, and all others will be left behind at the end of time, to face destruction in the apocalypse. You come from a fundamentalist Christian background, and you read the Bible every day, so what is your opinion of this belief?

God has not willed that any soul should perish. 900-20 When

opportunities are presented, it is the entity's own will force that must be exercised.... Hence, as for the entity's fulfilling its destiny, it is ever on the road. 903-23

So none of us needs to worry about being left behind, as some preachers claim?

God has not willed that any soul should perish but has with every temptation, with every condition prepared an association, an activity, a manner, a way for the regeneration of those influences or forces that may cause the overcoming of fear or any of those things that would separate a soul from the Creative Forces. 1646-1

You mean there is always a chance for us to redeem ourselves no matter what condition we have created in our rebellion?

With each condition that has arisen within the experience of the soul [He has] prepared a way, and these are a constant change being wrought. Not that through activities—of course, the time and the place and the position—but it is ever the choice of the individual. It is that which makes or is the godly force within an individual, or an entity or a soul, that makes it seek its level. 1602-3 Each soul is destined to become a portion of the First Cause, or back to its Maker. 987-2

How can we assure people that they will not be left behind?

In your activities, then, make the way known that the Christ loves every soul—and wills that none shall be lost. 281-19

Since the soul of each individual is part of the One Soul, the Great Soul, or what Ralph Waldo Emerson called the "Over-soul," what is meant by the phrase "a soul lesson," as if the soul instead of being our guide and destiny, needs to learn some lessons?

If the soul were at all periods, all manifestations, to keep in that perfect accord, or law, with the "Over-soul," or the First Cause, or the Soul from which it comes, then there would be only a continuous at-onement with the First Cause. But when an entity, a soul, uses a period of manifestation—in whatever realm of consciousness—to its *own indulgencies*, then there is need for the lesson, or for the soul understanding or interpreting, or to become aware of the error of its way. 815-7

In one of your readings, you said that a client (815) was selfish in his relations with a woman (2700). What did you advise him?

In your own experiences in the earth, in relationships with this entity, you possessed the body without regard to the unfoldment of the soul of this entity, in its relationships to the First Cause. Now: The lesson is, though in the *mind*, there are the needs for encouragement, love, the associations for the better activity of the body. Are these to be in mind or in reality, reality meaning soul? Hence a lesson becomes necessary. 815-7

Could he redeem himself?

As to whether it is to be rectified in this present experience depends upon choices taken in relationships to mental and material activities. As is oft expressed, the spirit is willing, the motivating force of a soul-entity is willing, but the body, ego, mind, the impelling force to or through which consciousness arises and makes the entity aware through the emotions of mind and body, has its lesson to gain. 815-7

Many people are preoccupied with themselves or with their own concerns. Is this wrong?

Self-glory, self-exaltation, self-indulgence are influences that become abominations to the divinity in each soul, and *separate* them from a knowledge of Him. For you are persuaded, for you *know* from your experience, *nothing* may separate the soul of man from its Maker but desires and lusts! 1293-1

How do we decide what is selfish and what is appropriate self-concern?

[When] the entity allows self to be drawn away from the first principles; so that it is *self* that wants to do something! This rather indicates the selfish nature, that is innate in an entity.

While each soul, each associate, each acquaintance *is* an obligation, a duty—all of these must cooperate, coordinate. As the body itself in its welfare, mentally, or physically, unless it cooperates, coordinates each portion with the other, there is not the well-rounded, the well-balanced individual nor the better and best reactions from same....

The spirit is the life. Then each phase of the experience of the entity must be of the spiritual import in its very nature, if it is to live, to be the fulfilling of its purpose—to bring peace and harmony, for which purpose it *is* in existence! It must be constructive in the very nature and the very desires, without thought of self being the one glorified in or by same! Rather the *glory* is to the influence or force what *prompts* same!

If even filial or marital or soul love seeks the exalting of self, then it is not fulfilling its purpose from the spiritual import. God is love! The influence or force that motivates the life of each soul is love! But it may be love of self, of fame, of fortune, of glory, of beauty, or of self-indulgence, self-aggrandizement, or the satisfaction to the ego! These are the conditions [or choices one makes] that *must* be in *every* phase of the experience analyzed....

Thus, whether it brings material hardships, material problems or not, such an ideal is to be held to; and the problems will be dissipated by the very influence and force of the love and the desire that is *purposeful* but *selfless* in its nature, in its activity!

And when this is applied, when this is done, when the activi-

ties are in that direction, we will find the channels for the abilities—the connections, the associations—will be as it were creative
in themselves. Not as show, but rather as what there may be the
magnifying of brotherly love and hope and promise and faith in a
creative force and influence! 1579-1

*But we are born pretty self-centered creatures, perhaps necessarily so as
a matter of self-preservation. But how do we transform ourselves from
self-centered to God-centered souls?*

We grow [gradually] in grace, in knowledge, [and] in understanding. 349-12

*Are we condemned or doomed by damnation or destruction if we don't
grow to Heaven by the time we die?*

The Father has not willed that any soul should perish, and is
mindful that each soul has again—and yet again—the opportunity for making its paths straight. 2021-1

*What happens to the soul if it fails to show the requisite development at
the end of the life cycle?*

It reincarnates, that it may have the opportunity [to improve].
826-8 The *soul* is not lost; the *individuality* of the soul that separated itself [from God] is lost. The reincarnation or the opportunities are continuous until the soul has of itself become an entity in
its whole. 826-8

*If we live only one lifetime, does that mean we were really good in God's
eyes?*

To find that you only lived [once], died, and were buried under
the cherry tree...does not make you one whit better than neighbor, citizen, mother, or father. But to know you spoke unkindly
and suffered for it, and in the present [life] may correct it by being
righteous, *that* is worth while. 5753-2

How often do we reincarnate before we achieve perfection?

Perfection is not possible in a material body until you have at least entered some thirty times. 2982-2

Is all of our soul growth dependent upon what we learn or how we behave toward others on earth, or does the soul develop in the afterlife as well?

Often the longer the periods between the earthly sojourns the greater has been—or may be—the development of the soul entity to that which each soul is to attain through its appearances [on earth].[59] 486-1

When we return for another life on earth, you say we may change gender or race?

At times. 136-27

This depends upon that experience necessary for the completion, for the building up of the purposes for which each and every soul manifests in the material experience.... The experiences of a soul entity in materiality... are as lessons or studies in that particular phase of the entity's or soul's development. 294-189

Some people have strong differences about when the mother's fertilized egg becomes a baby, a new human being. When does the soul enter the body of the child, at conception, or at birth, or when?

It may be at the first moment of breath [after the baby is delivered]; it may [be] some hours before birth; or many hours after birth. 457-10

In other words, it does not happen at the moment of conception. What keeps the baby living until the soul enters?

Spirit! For, the spirit of matter—its source is life, of God. 2390-2

---

59. An extended time gap between incarnations usually gives the soul an opportunity to mature before entering another incarnation on earth.

Is there always a soul available when a new baby is delivered?

Many souls are seeking to enter, but not all are attracted. Some may be repelled [by the difficulties they perceive]. Some are attracted and then suddenly repelled, so that their life in the earth is only a few days [possibly resulting in infant death]. 281-53

So the life cycle of the soul continues on into eternity?

Life and death are one, and only those who will consider the experience as one may come to understand or comprehend what peace indeed means. 1977-1 One is the birth of the other when viewed from the whole or the center. 369-3

∽

CHAPTER 15

A Path to Peace

WHILE WARS AND lesser forms of human violence have dominated the story of humankind, Cayce offers hope for the peace-
makers. Violence is not God's way, he says; and as the family of
nations crowds closer together on the planet, people can find
peace and harmony by giving up their quest for power and em-
phasizing their commonality, their brotherhood, rather than their
differences. Peace is not a vain hope but a necessity for the
human race to fulfill its destiny.

*We've talked a lot about ways to improve personal relations. What can
we do to improve relations between nations to prevent wars?*

Man's answer to everything has been power—power of money,
power of position, power of wealth, power of this, that, or the
other. This has never been God's way, will never be God's way.
3976-8

*Wasn't reliance on power ancient man's means of survival in the
wilderness, using it to subdue the earth, so to speak?*

Man—with his natural bent—not only attempted to subdue

the earth, but to subdue one another; and the result was the differences of opinions, the various sects, sets, classes, and races.

As the earth was peopled, and the abilities of expansion were able to bring the various groups, or associations of groups or nations, they *could*—and *did*—withdraw into themselves, and build for themselves in the various portions of the world that known as the periods of advancement of some particular group of peoples. 3976-8

Yes, today it is easy to forget that for centuries various peoples had little contact with other groups if they wished to remain isolated and at peace. Even the United States remained isolated behind the oceans until less than a century ago.

As the world has advanced, all the various phases of man's developments have entered to make a different phase, either in the political, economic, or religious aspect of man's experience. 3976-8

It is often said that times have changed in ways that influence our behavior, usually for the worse, often because life is not as simple as it once was for many of us. Is that a factor in world relations?

As has been and is being understood by many, there are changes being wrought in the nation, as well as in the inter[national] relationships with other nations. All of these may be considered from the one angle. It is also understood, comprehended by some, that a new order of conditions is to arise; that there must be many a purging in high places as well as low; that there must be the greater consideration of each individual, each soul being his brother's keeper. There will then come about those circumstances in the political, the economic, and the whole relationships where there will be a leveling—or a greater comprehension of this need.

For as the time or the period draws near for these changes that come with the new order, it behooves all of those who have an ideal—as individuals, as well as groups or societies or organizations—to be practicing, applying same in their experience and their relationships as one to another. For unless these are up and doing, then there must indeed be a new order in *their* relationships and their activities. For His ways will carry through. For as He gave, "Though the heavens and the earth may pass away, my word will not pass away."

All too often has this message been forgotten in the pulpits and in the organizations, not only in the national relationships but in the international relationships. And as the dealings are as one to another, unless these are in keeping with those tenets they must fail; for all power in Heaven and in earth hath been given into His hands.

Then as we approach all phases of human relationships, these must be taken into consideration. And there cannot be one measuring stick for the laborer in the field and the man behind the counter, and another for the man behind the money changers. All are equal—not only under the material law but under the spiritual. And His laws, His will, will not come to naught! 3976-18

Ever since the development of nation-states, conflicts across their borders have often led to military clashes, if not all-out war. Do you see any hope for settling such disputes peacefully?

Though there may come those periods when there will be great stress, as brother rises against brother, as group or sect or race rises against race—yet the leveling must come. And *only* those who have set their ideal in Him and practiced it in their dealings with their fellow man may expect to survive the wrath of the Lord.

In your dealings, then—whether at home, in your dealings with state or the national situations, or the international affairs—there must come all under that purpose, that desire. And then there should be, there will be those rising to power [who] are able to meet the needs. For none are in power but that have been given the opportunity by the will of the Father—from which all power emanates. Hence those will be leveled with the purpose, "My word shall not fail!" 3976-18

It seems like there is more violence than ever these days since the terrorist attacks of 9/11.

With the advent of the closeness of the worlds coming into being, so that the man upon the other side of the world is as much the neighbor as the man next door, more and more have been the turmoils that have arisen in the attempt of individual leaders or groups to induce, force, or compel one portion of the world to think as the other, or the other group to dwell together as brethren with one bond of sympathy, or one standard for all. 3976-8

The twentith century was dominated by two world wars and threats of a third, and the Middle East is in continuous turmoil, torn by war and suicide bombings. Are we destined to keep repeating these violent ideological struggles rather than be reconciled to our differences?

[The nations] have all come to that place in the development of the human family where there must be a reckoning, a one point upon which all may agree, that out of all of this turmoil that has arisen from the social life, racial differences, the outlook upon the relationship of man to the Creative Forces or his God, and his relationships one with another, must come to some *common* basis upon which all *may* agree. 3976-8

Many would say it is impractical to try to get such an agreement and impossible to achieve.

What has caused the present conditions, not alone at home but abroad? It is that realization that was asked some thousands of years ago, "Where *is* thy brother? His blood *cries* to me from the ground!" and the other portion of the world has answered, *is* answering, "Am I my brother's keeper?" The world, as a world—that makes for the disruption, for the discontent—has lost its ideal. Man may not have the same *idea*. Man—*all* men—may have the same *ideal!* 3976-8

In other words, we need to honor a common ideal, even though we have different ideas of how to achieve it. But Christians, Jews, and Muslims have been at odds for 2,000 years.

Have you not found that the *essence*, the truth, the *real* truth is one? Mercy and justice; peace and harmony. For without Moses and his leader Joshua (that was bodily Jesus) there *is* no Christ. Christ is not a man! Jesus was the man; Christ the messenger; Christ in all ages, Jesus in one, Joshua in another, Melchizedek in another; these be those that led Judaism! These be they that came as that child of promise, as to the children of promise; and the promise is in you, that you lead as He has given you, "Feed my sheep." 991-1

As the Spirit of God once moved to bring peace and harmony out of chaos, so must the Spirit move over the earth and magnify itself in the hearts, minds, and souls of men to bring peace, harmony, and understanding, that they may dwell together in a way that will bring that peace, that harmony, that can only come with all having the one Ideal; not the one idea, but "Thou shalt love the Lord Thy God with all thine heart, thy neighbor *as* thyself!" This [is] the whole law, this [is] the whole answer to the world, to each and every soul. That is the answer to the world conditions as they exist today. 3976-8

How can this be brought about?

As [they] each in their own respective sphere put into action what they know to be the fulfilling of what has been from the beginning, so does the little leaven leaven [ferment] the whole lump. Rather little by little, line upon line, here a little, there a little, each thinking rather of the other fellow, as that which has kept the world in the various ways of being intact—where there were ten, even, many a city, many a nation, has been kept from destruction.

Though you may look upon, or feel that what was given to Abram—as he viewed the cities of the plain and pled for the saving of same—was an allegorical story, a beautiful tale to be told children—that it might bring fear into the hearts of those [who] would have their *own* way—may it not come into the hearts of those now, today, will you, yourself, make of your *own* heart an understanding that you must answer for your own brother, for your own neighbor!

And who is your neighbor? He that lives next door, or he that lives on the other side of the world? He, rather, that is in *need* of understanding! He who has faltered; he who has fallen even by the way. *He* is your neighbor, and you must answer for him! 3976-8

What do you say to critics of this idealistic prescription who say it is a pipedream?

Do you have ideals spiritually? Do you desire that you may be controlled of power and might, or do you desire power and might that you may glorify your Maker?

Determine these in yourself; not merely by saying "Yes, I'll be a good boy." But live it for a year, and come around, sonny, and we'll tell you. 3618-1

But we've had idealistic leaders such as Woodrow Wilson, who advocated the League of Nations as a means of reconciling conflicts between nations instead of resorting to war. Why didn't it make a difference?

Such conditions have been the dream of many an individual, and of many with much more material power and prestige than those who would consider such at the present. Same was the idea of Alexander [the Great] when he sought to conquer the world, yet the tenets of the ideal were forgotten in the desires of the flesh, and while the principles as set forth in the mind and heart of the man as the student under Plato and Archimedes, and Aurilius and others, the *man* became so gored by the greed of power as to become the loathsome body—as it passes to its reward for the use of the power as given into the hands....

Only in Him in whom there was found no guile, and though He were buffeted by man—though He was ridiculed by those in power, though He suffered among those convicted of crime in the flesh, and railings against their fellow man—yet those tenets were proclaimed by that as the man, making self as the son of man, and through those conditions became the Son of the living God— in these tenets, in *these* ways and manners, may such conditions be brought to the realization of those that would *build* an invisible empire within the hearts of men; and seeking then the way for each one as would head each organization as would be necessary, there would be seen that in a short while there may be brought into realization that that would be able to rule—*not* as an iron rule of the oppressor; not as one seeking to subjugate others to the will—but *making* the will one with that universal force necessary to bring everyone to that throne of grace, of faith, of hope, of love, of *all* those conditions necessary to build hospitals, churches, roads, loans, and help others to help themselves. 3976-4

How can we build such a following?

First the choosing of those who would give self in holy communion with this one purpose and, making self right with God, choose to be used as an *instrument* of Good for the saving of the Good in human principles; for...the world awaits the coming of those who will proclaim the day of freedom from the bonds of those who would rule, either through prestige or through political influence, see?

Then, ones so chosen by their fitness—as will come through such communion—will be the first to begin. See? For, as each are chosen, through these same forces there may be given their perfect fitness for such elements; . . . let's give to each their place, their niche, their abilities, their conditions, concerning such ideals. To some these are ideals that may be used, see, for their own personal gains. To others these are ideals that will be benefits to the world, see? We are speaking of individuals, as individuals.

In [such a person] there is found first that necessity of making self's inner self one with that creative energy that would make an answer of "My spirit beareth witness with thy Spirit, O God, that I am thy Son, and willing to be used as an instrument of Good toward the giving of mankind the opportunity to know the will of thy Son as may be manifest through *my* activities toward my fellow man, in carrying out that which will become the crowning glory of *my* life, and my service to my fellow man; laying aside those things that so easily beset, and I will run the race as is set before me in Him!" 3976-4

What place does such a person's religion play in this goal?

Keep each not as religion, but as the dictates of the heart to guide, direct, the fellow man—for before each there is set a way, and in that way is set a light. Veer not from same! Let him that is weak of mind or heart not take the handle, for he that plows and looks back is worse than the infidel. 3976-4

World peace eludes us when nations can't solve their conflicts without resorting to violence and justifying it in terms of self-defense.

It is, then, still the challenge to each country, to each nation, that while there is, to be sure, the natural instinct or purpose of self-preservation, it is to be less and less of self and more and more for that which was from the beginning. Then, there needs be that not so much be set as to this ritual, or this form, or the other, for any given peoples or any nation, but rather that the individuals in each nation, *everywhere*, are to turn again to the God of the fathers and not in self-indulgence, self-aggrandizement, but more and more of self-effacement. For as the people of each nation pray, *and* then live that prayer, so must the Spirit work.

Then—each of you here—*give God a chance* to show what great blessings He will give to those who love Him. This does not mean that you, or *anyone*, would condone persecutions anywhere or in any form. For, you know His laws fail not—"As ye sow, so shall ye reap."

Man can only begin, then, within himself. And as he applies what he knows, what he understands of God, in his daily life, so may there be given him the next step to make. 3976-23

The trouble is most leaders of nations believe they must take a traditional "my country, right or wrong" approach and do whatever they think is in their country's immediate best interest, or their own political interest, without regard for the interest of other peoples.

As they attempt to preserve their own personalities, their own selves, without thought of their fellow man, they may succeed for the moment, but "God is not mocked," and whatsoever a man, a country, a nation sows, that it must reap.

"What then," you ask, "is to be the outcome? What is there that I can do about it?"

Let your daily life be free from criticism, from condemnation, from hate, from jealousy. And as you give power to the Spirit of Peace, so may the *Prince of Peace*, the love of God, manifest. So long as you turn your thoughts to the manners and means for meeting and overcoming those destructive forces, you show forth that which may bring to the world that day of the Lord. For the promise is that in the latter days there shall be the purposes in the *hearts* of men, everywhere!

There *is* in every land today—through the prayers that have gone up—a more seeking for that at-onement with [the] Creative Forces, a more seeking for the knowledge and the purposes of God, than there has been for ages.

Then, rest not on those things that become quicksand about you, but on the true, the tried arm of God. For the earth is His, and the fullness thereof. 3976-23

Do you think people would respond to such a high calling?

Many peoples—in many nations, in many climes—are ready and willing to follow that Light, that Star. 3976-4

Don't people often rely on power out of fear instead of following their ideals?

Fear is the root of most of the ills of mankind, whether of self, or of what others think of self, or what self will appear to others. Fear [is] the greatest bugaboo to the human elements, for in fear comes those conditions that destroy that vitality of that assimilated. 5439-1

What can we as individuals do to contribute to peace?

Whatever is necessary to make one's self wholly in accord with what you know to be the correct attitude toward self, family, neighbor, associates—social and business—and keep self unspotted from censure by your own conscience. 5459-3

Learn first that lesson of cooperation. Become less and less selfish, and more and more selfless in Him. Be not afraid to be made fun of to become aware of His presence, that self may be a channel through which the glory of the Father may come unto men in a manner that all may know there is a glory, even an Israel, of the Lord.

Be patient, long-suffering, bearing one another's burdens. Be joyous in the Lord. Be not tempestuous in manner, thought, act, or deed; rather *serving* in humbleness of spirit. Enjoy your labors.

Enjoy those things that make for the unison of thought in Him. 262-29

What do you say to those who believe that idealistic, selfless people will only be taken advantage of at every turn?

Look for Good and you will find it. Search for it, for it is as a pearl of great price. For there is so much Good in the *worst*, that you may never judge another by your own short standards. Condemn not if you would not be condemned. 1776-1

Many people are afraid to be kind, to be open, to love others. And yet people were created with a capacity to fear, I suppose, to protect themselves from physical dangers. Is it not reasonable to respect one's fears?

Fear is the fruit of indecisions respecting that which is lived and that which is held as the ideal. Doubt is the father of fear. Remember, as He gave, "He that asks in my name, doubting not, shall have; for I go to the Father." If doubt has crept in, it becomes as the father of fear. Fear is the beginning of faltering. Faltering makes for dis-ease throughout the soul and mental body. 538-33

Selfishness is what makes men afraid. The awareness of the necessities of the carnal forces in a material world seeking their gratification. Don't you know that whether you live or die you live or die in the Lord? As He gave, "If thine eye offend, pluck it out. If thine hand lead thee in error, cut it off."

When one has set the ideal, and knows what the ideal represents, and then knows self measured by the ideal, one sees, is aware of what is lacking or what is overdone in self, and plucks it out, and beholds not the mote that is in his brother's eye but considers rather the beam that is in his own eye. 262-29

How do we overcome fear to follow our higher angels?

To *overcome* fear, so fill the mental forces with that of the creative nature as to cast out fear; for he, or she, that is without fear is free indeed, and perfect love casts out fear. Love not that is of the officious nature, or that which demands in exchange. Rather [love] given as the free will, and *making* the will one with what will enable the body mental to see, [to] experience, to know, to feel, that nearer and nearer the will of the body made one with that the body worships—and let that worshipfulness be of *other* than of self; for *many* a body stumbles and blinds self by putting self first and foremost. 5439-1

In the matter of worry, this—in its last analysis—is fear. Fear is an enemy to the mental development of an entity, changing or wavering the abilities of an entity in many directions. 2502-1

[And] remember the injunction—never worry as long as you can pray. When you can't pray—you'd better begin to worry! For then you have something to worry about! 3569-1

The Cayce Metaphysical Cosmology

CAYCE MADE NO attempt to skew the information he received clairvoyantly to make it fit a predetermined philosophy, even when it breached the borders of the Christian doctrine he learned as a boy. The belief system that emerged in his readings never varied. His source, you might say, remained true. Although Cayce never proclaimed his concepts as a philosophy, they certainly constitute a coherent body of thought, a Cayce metaphysical cosmology, if you will. Its tenets, distilled from the preceding interviews, follow.

The Creative Forces that produced the universe developed a plan from the Mind of God by which our solar system, along with countless other galaxies, was created in preparation for God's highest creation: a spirit in His own likeness. God created souls out of His desire for companionship. The pattern for these souls was that of God Himself as found in spirit, mind, and individual free will.

Given free will, however, some souls developed a taste for independence and focused more on their own creations than those of God. Souls became intrigued with matter and found their way into the physical realm of earth by way of a creature that offered sanctuary. Through the influence of the soul, these creatures gave earth a new inhabitant: primitive man. This evolutionary development occurred in different regions of the planet, thus resulting in the separate races.

Originally, souls were androgynous. But now they were a part of male and female individuals, and they soon discovered that sex between the two genders and reproduction of the species was the only way for other souls to join them on earth.

God, having provided free will, does nothing to prevent Man from exercising it in violation of His laws. He provides for a reconciliation, however, once Man has finished asserting his independence outside the ways and will of God. It is a plan for a cycle of multiple incarnations in earth during which Man has an opportunity to mature spiritually, cast off carnal impulses, and eventually become aligned with God.

Between incarnations, the wandering soul experiences other planetary influences designed to bring it back in line with the Creator. The law of karma governs the progress of each soul, overseeing any debt that must be repaid for past misdeeds.

In this respect, Cayce's philosophy owes much to the ancient religious doctrines of the Orient. But, as his biographer Thomas Sugrue states, it is "a Christianized version of the mystery religions of ancient Egypt, Chaldea, Persia, India, and Greece. It fits the figure of Christ into the tradition of one God for all people, and places Him in His proper place, at the apex of the philosophical structure; He is the capstone of the pyramid."[60]

The Christ, appearing on earth through several righteous Old Testament figures such as Joshua and Joseph, had completed its cycle and returned to God, only to volunteer to return to earth to show Man the way back to God. Thus arrived Jesus of Nazareth,

60. Sugrue, *There Is a River.*

who offered the pattern we are all to follow. Our souls' purpose is to find our way home no matter how many lifetimes it takes. Our souls, which are the God part of us, never die. Nor do we face any fires of Hell other than those we create for ourselves by piling up karmic debts. Such trials and tribulations that we encounter along the way are learning experiences that refine the soul. Paradise, the reunion with God, awaits those who learn to love God and their neighbor as themselves.

No soul will be left behind.

Glossary

Cayce often used unorthodox terms or descriptive metaphors to explain his concept of life in both the physical and spiritual realms. The meaning of some terms is apparent, but others are more difficult to fathom. Here is a selection of terms he often used and my interpretation of their meaning:

Active or **Activative Force**—God did not just create the universe but remains an Active or Activating Force in the working of His creation on every level.

Afterlife—The spiritual existence into which the soul moves when a physical incarnation ends in death.

Angel—Cayce expanded on the biblical description of angels as messengers from God to humankind, saying every soul has an angel assigned to it to offer guidance and protection during its journey. Like a friend in court, the angel serves as that soul's advocate "before the Throne of the First Cause."

Astral travel—The soul's journey periodically involves astral travel, which is movement among the stars, including any of the planets that offer influences favorable to the soul's development. Such sojourns may occur during periods when the body to which the soul is attached is sleeping or when the soul has been released from the body of the deceased.

Astral plane—The space in the universe in which the soul travels.

Atomidine—An iodine compound recommended by Cayce for arthritis and certain skin conditions.

At-onement—The term suggests an accord as opposed to a division between humans and God. It is a play on the theological term *atonement*, meaning a reconciliation between humans and God.

Body—Beyond the customary usage for a physical form, Cayce may use it to mean "somebody" or "the person." He also uses it as a hyphenated expression with soul or mental (soul-body or mind-body) to suggest that these nonphysical aspects of a person also are a body of sorts.

Book, or **The Book**—The Bible.

Borderland—The spirit world outside the physical realm in which we live on earth contains numerous realms, starting with the borderland that is closest to the earth and through which the soul passes following the death of a body. Spirits that remain in the borderland for extended periods are said to be overly attached to the physical plane.

Christ—"That universal consciousness of love that we see manifested in those who have forgotten self" as Jesus did, and who "give themselves that others may know the truth," said Cayce.

Christ-consciousness—The latent awareness within each soul of oneness with God, waiting to be awakened and manifested in each life.

Cosmic—Having to do with the farthest expanses of the universe, including both spiritual and physical realms.

Creative Forces—One of several metaphors for God.

Creator—God.

Destiny—What a soul does with its will in relationship to God.

Devil—The personification of Evil.

Divine within—To the extent that each person is made "in the image of God," as the Bible says, it is the soul that reflects the Divine within, or God.

Drosses—Waste products formed in the body.

Earth plane—The physical realm on earth as distinct from other cosmic or spiritual planes or realms of existence.

Entity—Most often a person who is the subject of the reading he is giving, whether referring to that entity in the present life or a past life or in the spirit world.

Fear of the Lord—Deep reverence and awe at the majesty of God.

First Cause—A metaphor for God.

Fourth Dimension—A description, possibly metaphorical, for those cosmic or spiritual realms beyond earth's three-dimensional plane.

Free will—At the time of Creation, God endowed each soul with free will, which is the capacity to make choices independent of the will or guidance of other souls and the Creator.

Fruits of the Spirit—An expression attributed to the apostle Paul for those acts and attributes of a person who is at one with God, such as loving, kindness, generosity, long-suffering.

God or **Lord God**—The Supreme Being, the Creator and Ruler of the universe.

God is One—There is only one deity, whatever name individual religions may choose to use.

God's other door—A metaphor for death, or the passage of the soul at the time of the demise of the physical body.

Grace—The unmerited kindness, mercy, and forgiveness shown by God.

Guardian angel—See Angel.

Holy Spirit—God's presence among us.

Ideals—Goals set by a person for mental, physical, and spiritual objectives designed to elevate or transform one spiritually toward a higher state of awareness, ultimately Christ-consciousness.

Interim—The period between earthly incarnations during which the soul is engaged on the other side.

Individuality—The personality of our soul or inner self as distinct from our outer self, or the personality we project to others.

Incarnation—A single physical life on earth. A soul's return to earth in a new body is a reincarnation.

Jesus—The man who embodied the pattern for living a God-centered, rather than self-centered, life and promised, as Cayce said, "whosoever loveth me and keepeth my commandments, to him will I come—and I will abide with him."

Karma—Like cause and effect, karma brings consequences as a result of deeds affecting others. It can be negative karma for hurts to others or positive for good deeds. Unlike cause and effect, which is confined to the physical world, karma operates in the spiritual realms as well and may extend through multiple incarnations.

Karmic debt—Spiritual obligations to make amends for nonconstructive past behavior.

Karmic credit—Benefits gained from having been of service to others.

Kundalini—An energy that develops in the pelvic region of the body and, under certain conditions such as meditation, may rise up the spinal column to provide an altered state of consciousness. Such episodes are often accompanied by visions or other mystical experiences.

Law—Unlike statutory law made, amended, or repealed by humans to guide their conduct on earth, Cayce speaks of universal spiritual laws as commandments much like the writers of the Bible did, laws concerning Love and Truth that come from the Creator and are unchangeable.

Lord—Jesus the Christ.

Manifestation—An expression of life in the physical realm on earth.

Master—Jesus the Christ.

Materiality—Usually pertains to the physical world, including the physical body, and what the soul experiences during its journey through the earth plane.

Messiah—A Hebrew term meaning "Anointed One" (translated in the Greek to "Christ") for the long-awaited savior to deliver the Jews.

Mind—The mental aspect of a person responsible for thinking, remembering, choices of the will, and the seat of human consciousness.

Mind-body—A metaphor for the human mind.

One God—The deity, by whatever name any individual religion may prefer, is the same.

Oneness—Pertains to the interconnection of all that God created, including all races whose disparate members, being children of God, are brothers and sisters; and our connection with the earth and its natural resources and sentient beings.

Personality—That aspect of us that we display or project to the world, as distinct from individuality, which is our inner self or the personality of our soul.

Plane—A level of cosmic existence, as in the physical realm of earth or the spiritual realms in the universe beyond earth.

Pharoah—Ruler of Egypt.

Reading—When Cayce entered a self-induced hypnotic state and responded to questions posed by the person conducting the session, usually his wife, Gertrude, every word was recorded and his secretary later typed up a verbatim copy of everything that was said. This document came to be called a reading. There are over 14,000 such readings in the files of the Edgar Cayce Foundation at Virginia Beach, Virginia.

Scripture—The Bible.

Self—Cayce referred to the self that is guided by physical desires and mental choices, as well as a spiritual, or higher, self that serves as a guide, conscience, or guardian angel devoid of narrow physical or emotional cravings.

Sin—Disobeying God's commandments.

Sixth sense—A state of high awareness in an individual while asleep that serves the dream process.

Soul-body—A metaphor for the human soul.

Spirit—Designates the active force of the spiritual realms, or God, that may be evident in the physical or earth plane as well.

Spiritual plane—Nonphysical realms of the universe in which Spirit rules and souls evolve between incarnations in the earth plane.

Third-dimensional—Whatever pertains to life on earth or in materiality is limited to and described in three dimensions.

Universal laws or **Immutable laws**—See Law. Like cause and effect in the physical world, there are spiritual commandments or conditions with certain inescapable reactions or consequences.

Word—Referring to the word of God, meaning God's will or purposes revealed in laws and teachings. Jesus was also referred to as the Word of God (John 1:1).

Bibliography

Baldwin, William J. *Healing Lost Souls: Releasing Unwanted Spirits from Your Energy Body*. Charlottesville, VA: Hampton Roads, 2003.

Bro, Harmon H. *Edgar Cayce on Dreams*, New York: Hawthorne, 1968.

Cayce, Edgar. *My Life as a Seer: The Lost Memoirs*. Edited by A. Robert Smith. New York: Saint Martin's Press, 1997.

The Complete Edgar Cayce Readings. CD-ROM for Windows. Virginia Beach, VA: A.R.E. Press, 2004.

Davis, Adelle. *How to Cook It Right*. New York: Harcourt Brace Jovanovich, 1947.

Edgar Cayce's Diet and Recipe Guide. Virginia Beach, VA: A.R.E. Press, 1999.

Fiore, Edith. *The Unquiet Dead: A Psychologist Treats Spirit Possession*. Garden City, NY: Doubleday, 1987.

Gabbay, Simone. *Nourishing the Body Temple*. Virginia Beach, VA: A.R.E. Press, 2000.

———.*Visionary Medicine*. Virginia Beach, VA: A.R.E. Press, 2003.

Grant, Robert J. *The Place We Call Home*. Virginia Beach, VA: A.R.E. Press, 2000.

Johnson, K. Paul. *Edgar Cayce in Context*. Albany: State University of New York Press, 1998.

Kirkpatrick, Sidney. *Edgar Cayce: An American Prophet*. New York: Riverhead books, 2000.

McArthur, Bruce. *Your Life: Why It Is the Way It Is and What You Can Do about It*. Virginia Beach, VA: A.R.E. Press, 2000.

McGarey, William A. *The Cayce Remedies*. New York: Bantam, 1984.

Mein, Eric. *Keys to Health*. New York: Saint Martin's Press, 1989.

Moody, Raymond, Jr. *Life after Loss: The Investigation of a Phenomenon—Survival of Bodily Death*. Harrisburg, PA: Stockpole Books, 1976.

Ritchie, George. *Ordered to Return: My Life after Dying*. Charlottesville, VA: Hampton Roads, 1998.

Sechrist, Elsie. *Dreams: Your Magic Mirror*. Virginia Beach, VA: A.R.E. Press, 2000.

Stearn, Jess. *Edgar Cayce: The Sleeping Prophet*. New York: Doubleday, 1967.

Stevenson, Ian. *Twenty Cases Suggestive of Reincarnation*. Charlottesville: University of Virginia Press, 1974.

Sugrue, Thomas. *There Is a River*. New York: Holt, 1943.

Thurston, Mark. *Discovering Your Soul's Purpose*. Virginia Beach, VA: Edgar Cayce Foundation, 1984.

Todeschi, Kevin J. *Edgar Cayce on Soul Mates: Unlocking the Dynamics of Soul Attraction*. Virginia Beach, VA: A.R.E. Press, 1999.

Weiss, Brian L. *Many Lives, Many Masters*. New York: Warner Books, 1996.

Index

About the Editor

A. ROBERT SMITH is the compiler and editor of Edgar Cayce's memoirs, *Edgar Cayce: My Life as a Seer,* and the author of five other works of nonfiction, including *Misdiagnosed: Was My Wife a Casualty of America's Medical Cold War?*

An American Journalism Society award-winning journalist, he is the founding editor of *Venture Inward* magazine, an international periodical published by the Association for Research and Enlightenment that focuses on spirituality, mystical experiences, and holistic health, and has written for the *New York Times Magazine* and other national publications. He lives in Virginia Beach, Virginia.